To Tell The Truth:
The Final Clinton Scandal
A
Story of
Deceit, Denial and Defiance

To Tell The Truth:
The Final Clinton Scandal
A
Story of
Deceit, Denial and Defiance

By

Jerry E. Kletke

1st books – rev. 5/09/01

Dedicated to my son. May he be safe and know that his father loves him. And to my daughter, who told me what it is like to grow up without a father.

About To Tell The Truth

Hillary Rodham Clinton has a secret sister, Anna Couceiro, in Miami, Florida, who is a psychiatric nurse with the government. The author dated her in 1992-93, and she kept the birth of their son, Shawn a secret. The Clintons were going to "adopt" him and bring him into the White House after the 1996 election. Then the father found out, so the Clintons used CIA doctors to stop him with Hillary's mother and sister committing perjury.

This struggle with the Clintons and Hillary's family gives a real insight into Hillary's family with more deception and defiance of authority. This was a precursor to the Paula Jones deposition with no sexual relation and no male child claimed under oath. The authorities and CIA have been used to keep the father quiet while she sold cocaine to the same doctors. After years of effort, the Clintons still want to raise Shawn without the father, but the story is finally coming out. The hospital where Anna works even put implants in both of Shawn's father's ears to monitor and control him. The FBI and Secret Service has investigated the claims, but the White House continues to misuse CIA to stop the press and threaten him. How much trouble are the Clintons in now? Could this be their final scandal?

The author was in contact with the Clintons and Congress before and during the impeachment. Read his account of that historic event with the insight of this secret struggle taking place in the background.

Table of Contents

Appendices

Foreword

White House Abuse of Power

To Tell The Truth is an account of my relationship with Anna Couceiro, Hillary's sister, the Clintons and some of their other scandals, including Paula Jones, Kathleen Willey, China funds and the impeachment. My relationship involves the hiding of my son and preventing me from seeing him or even acknowledging I have a son. Doctors have told me that they are with the Central Intelligence Agency and have, over the years, been in contact with the President. More and more this is becoming a case of misuse of the Central Intelligence Agency directed by the White House.

I have questioned one how they could do this. Over the phone, her response was following orders. And, most recently, Dr. Weingrod admitted she lied to have me hospitalized to stop my book on the Clintons. In order to get released I had to tell authorities I had a tape recording of the visit. But the truth is coming out and the press now knows I had a boy with Anna Couceiro. This was necessary because I was told right after the 1996 campaign by Dr. A. Cohen that the Clintons wanted to raise my son without me, even if he felt differently. He would hospitalize me if the President requested it. Then came the false statement in writing to the court and the perjury by Anna and Hillary's mother. Prior to that they were in contact with the Clintons by phone. This forced me to write and expose this injustice. Besides the threats, the hospitalizations and excess medication, the Clintons have told the press not to report on me at all. I know of specific instances of Janet Reno and Hillary doing exactly this.

The doctors would not tell me how and when they were going to remove the batteries from the implants in both my ears implanted during a 1994 hospitalization at Jackson by doctors who worked with Anna and were keeping my son a secret. I decided to disclose their existence. I discovered them in early 1996 and partially disabled them by breaking the plastic wires just under my skin coming out of each ear. My private doctor at the time was Dr. Glassman. He said, he knows they could hear me. But can you hear anything? I told him it seems like it at times and he responded "that's too much." I was hospitalized soon after breaking the wires. I asked for a writ of habeas corpus and I was released from Jackson without them being able to refit me. They knew then that I had also found out about Shawn. I transferred to an H.M.O. where Dr. Carter and Dr. Masters took a scan of my head. Dr. Carter told me he saw where I had broken the wires and they could stay but that the batteries would eventually have to be removed. This was in 1996. I have kept quiet about this as being concerned with my son. But now I have gone public with this additional C.I.A. misconduct and would be surprised if it was not approved or even requested directly by the White House. On Thanksgiving in 1996 Anna made a reference to how she lets my son watch "Star Trek" and tells Shawn that his father is Data. "Watch how they keep taking parts of his brain in and out." She will throw C.I.A. at you too. And tried to have me Baker-Acted in person that very visit by the Hollywood police, saying she never had a child by me.

In late 1992 and early 1993, I dated Anna Couceiro, Hillary's sister, in Miami. She did not tell me she was pregnant when we broke up. I found out in late 1995 by accident. Bill and Hillary had already made plans to adopt him. As they stated publicly in the 1996 campaign, they would adopt a baby and bring it to the White House. I have also been told that the Clintons would raise my son completely without me and have been warned and threatened by various doctors to not ever say I have a son. Even though some of these doctors express that this was not their personal opinion, it is clear the doctors at Jackson, while treating me, kept him a secret and me from seeing a private doctor, Dr. Glassman of Around the Clock. He would help me off the excess medication the Jackson doctors were giving me since 1994. He was aware they had me picked up (Baker-Acted) for non-medical reasons at least once in 1994 and again in 1996, and now in 1999.

In 1993 around Thanksgiving and about the time my son must have been born, I received a call from President Clinton. He said he had papers on his desk about me. We talked for a short time. He suggested he might have work in Washington, but made then or not until late 1995 or early 1996, after I found out any reference to my son. He must have known of Shawn then and the purpose of the call might have been to get me out of Miami where, with contacts at Jackson, I might have found out about Shawn.

On or about July 4, 1996, Mrs. Clinton and I talked on the phone, and she said she was going to have Metro pick me up. The police came at 3:30 a.m. to take me to a mental hospital at her request. One of the many people at my front door at the time said that I had been writing the White House and this was the response. The new doctors told a representative of the old doctors from Jackson where Anna worked that the Clintons wanted Anna and me to get together and that the medication they had me on had ruined years of my life. The blood test alone would tell them I should not be on their medication, very heavy tranquilizers and memory blockers. But within weeks, I went to my physical and the 1996 campaign was over. Dr. A. Cohen told me the Clintons wanted to raise my son without me. And if the President told him to put me in a hospital, he would.

Within a few months, I went to court. Both Anna and her Mother went to the judge to have me hospitalized, saying there had been no relationship out of the hospital and that this was proof that I was ill. The judge refused and I proved in court at least a relationship. Their written response to the court states, there was no relationship out of the hospital. Then they both said "no" under oath, that Anna never gave birth to a male child. The judge knew differently but did not award me visitation or child support. I would need to find an attorney for him to work with. He liked one of the attorneys I had approached. But that attorney told me she was pressured, so she would not represent me in court.

Over six months later, I got a letter from her saying that she was not my attorney and that I should not contact her. I had just sent roses again to Anna and Shawn.

About this time (mid-1997) I decided to bring up my son to my doctor with Humana. She said there was a coverup and I better not say I had a son or they would kill me on the operating table. I wrote this up and sent it to the F.B.I. and then to her office. I got a new doctor as I requested.

With no witness and my being on the record, I decided to start tape recording my doctor's visits. On February 4, 1999, during one of my regular doctor's visits. I told her I was planning to return to court to see my son with the revenues from my book about this matter and some of the other Clinton scandals. She said I needed to be in a hospital. I disagreed, made an appointment for the next month, and then when home and made some phone calls to the Republican Party and another doctor to try and stop the Baker-Act. I decided to call Dr. Weingrod myself and her office told me to come back immediately. When I did, the police were there. She was telling them that I physically threatened them.

The first thing I told the police was that this was a trick and I asked to file a police report, claiming she was filing a false police report. I stated that I had made a tape recording of the entire visit. It would support my claim of not treating them in any way, shape or form. I was also interviewed several times at the hospital. They take threats very seriously and can be used to put you away for a long time much longer than a hospitalization when a doctor claims you just need your medication adjusted. Within a few days, Dr. Shapiro told me the doctor had admitted I had not threatened her and the real reason was to stop my book about the Clintons. The tape also has a discussion of the implants in my ears. In an earlier visit thay told me not to tell anyone, because they have other people with them.

So we had the various doctors that the White House and Anna have been in contact with. She not only knew many at Jackson but told me she has called the ones at Humana my H.M.O.. I distanced myself by joining the H.M.O. but they network. Some doctors were against Anna. She had sold them cocaine and been asked to stop by the F.B.I. in 1996 and then in January 1997 by Judge Greene. I was told that a man using her address had been picked up with cocaine on him in 1997 and she will be arrested if she goes back to it. Her mother told me she knew I wanted her to stop and not go to jail. But that is where her money is going according to a Christmas 1997 phone conversation. Anna wanted me to get into that in 1993 and got very upset when I refused. The hospital that hired her, Jackson, was well aware of this. Since the late 1970s I had been told several times by people from Washington that there is a problem with cocaine and they like me because they knew I wanted nothing to do with it.

The abuse of overmedication by Dr. Matista, in the early and mid-1990s that works with Anna. And sent people to go through my home. Removing evidence on more than one occasion she has also said she is with the C.I.A. In 1994, they put me under at Jackson for the whole weekend.

After filing my nails a little better to start going around to offices with computer work I had just completed and while scratching the back of my head in the shower I found a string or wire under my skin. In the following days and weeks, I was able to take pins, go under the skin and pull out the white thin plastic wires and cut or break them. I counted 10 when doing my right ear. Drs. Carter and Roskin of Humana confirm this. And Dr. Weingrod also knows this and told me not to tell anyone because they have other people. The device in my right ear does not work and the left ear has now gotten weak. They could really work you with them both going. I took a sample of a half inch piece and put in a envelope, but it was gone after I returned from Jackson.

Since 1995, I have written and called U.S. congressional offices on this matter, and about my son Shawn. I am asking for simple visitation under the guidelines of the Florida Statutes. Lawyers I have spoken with over the years tell me my book which is now finished and off to 50 political publishers and e-mailed to political talk shows, is the best way to address this. It will give me the means to raise my son and get Anna in a townhouse. I am now waiting for the story to break the local newspapers now that they believe me or recognize Hillary has a sister and that there is a boy.

Back in November 1996, after the elections were over I asked the White House to please just give me the birth date of my son so I knew there was some hope of working this out. When they refused, I sent the first part of To Tell The Truth to every U.S. senator and about 150 congressional offices that have e-mail. The leadership was already aware of the White House's involvement in hiding my son and taking steps to stop me from seeing him. According to one congressional office, it may very well be why the doctor had me hospitalized in February 1999. Basically this is ongoing misuse of the C.I.A. directed by the White House.

Back in 1989, I took a Jackson doctor to court for just a thousand dollars. They put me in a long-term mental hospital for this. It is true that these doctors, as they mostly treat the ill and often those that are not even fit to take care of themselves, do get involved in intelligence. It seems like they are acting under orders in this matter.

It is an interesting note that in January of 1990, after working at the Bay Club in Miami and just completing a computer program for Jackson Memorial's new-to-be trauma center, I found myself tricked in to Janet Reno's Dade county jail. I was at the entrance and a lady in a white lab coat said, "We want to talk to you upstairs."

The Dade County State Attorney's office is on the eleventh floor and they had represented the doctor in my civil lawsuit that had ended six months prior. I had sent Janet Reno's attorneys an account of my relationship with Jackson as background on my complaint. At the last hearing, she had sent her assistant to defend the doctor. The lady stopped the elevator on the floor below, a section of the jail where medication was passed out. I had been captured again, and in the cell area was a man with hundreds of U.S. dollars under his mattress. The entire underside was covered and they were sticking out around the sides. I noticed no one dollar bills.

He was there for committing credit card fraud and was continuing his profession in jail. The guards would let him use the phone to order merchandise for them. This was reported eventually years later by "60 Minutes" and the Miami Herald just before Janet Reno became Attorney General. I sent in letters about it, once it broke. It was common for public defenders of Janet Reno to go into the very cell area on a regular basis. But this just continued on for years. Sometimes they need help from a writer. Her office picked up charges on me and the higher up of the very doctor I had taken to court shipped me off to a long-term detention and health care facility.

Apparently they were so impressed with my writing that they refused to process me until I agreed to work for them. They got to like you. I got a call from Janet Reno in 1996 and she told me I was all mixed up again (a pause then) with important people. I was blessed and able to talk to Hillary in the same call. Then Bill told me he was putting them in charge of me. But I haven't heard since, not even from my liberal sister.

Introduction

In late summer of 1992, Bill and Hillary Clinton were out front. I had called the Democratic Party in Miami, Florida, to perform volunteer work. Before the call was returned I was taken the next morning by police to Jackson Memorial Hospital, Baker-Acted as a mental patient, only to find Hillary's sister worked there and was in her third year of a two-year student nursing program. I had been to Jackson before and I was 100 percent when I was picked up. Had the government stopped me from becoming more politically involved? Or did they like me and want me to met Anna? Or was this just another coincidence?

We got to know each other and dated out of the hospital. She would call me so I would not get in trouble. Our relationship lasted only a few months but with a pregnancy that was kept, from me. I had been given a small television, some old clothes and a refrigerator from her mother. I did not tell anyone about my relationship with the now First Lady's sister. The next contact was a phone call from the President in 1993, about the time unknownst to me that our son was born. He had papers on his desk about me. I asked if this call was because the two hundred or so men in the North Wing of the White House were giving him trouble. He said no. I read the legal definition of capacitance from a legal dictionary I had recently picked up. He was impressed and slightly amused. I never addressed him but talked to him like we were old friends. He started to hint that I might be interested in working in Washington. It was all I needed to hear and hung up. I had been there before and was not interested.

Over a year went by and the President and First Lady were visiting Miami. I got caught in traffic because of the

Presidential motorcade. As it went by Mrs. Clinton, who I had never met before, noticed my car, a very large white automobile with red top and twenty years old. She pointed it out to Bill and he moved forward to look. I wonder again what the interest could be but was glade to forget. I had become a Republican after dating her sister Anna and was not interested in them. It was late 1995 and the Clintons were visiting Miami a lot. I would tell people they had friends and family here as if I was pretending to know them.

On a drive past a park that Anna and I had gone to, I saw Anna walking a child along the wall. It was my son! Now these trips to Miami and Hillary saying they were going to adopt a baby and bring it to the White House after the 1996 elections had meaning to me. I had become another person involved in a dispute with them. Hopefully, it could be resolved in private and to everyone's benefit. But it was already at the point of deceit and it led first to denial and then to defiance.

This is an account of my relationship with Hillary's family in Miami and some of the other more public scandals of this administration. With the land fraud scheme know as Whitewater and the persistent claims of Paula Jones, the Clintons were on their way to reelection in 1996. I find myself a father and had just started sending in jokes for David Letterman of "Late Night" fame. The liberals had found their way back into my life. To Tell The Truth will walk though the Paula Jones dispute and the Monica Lewinsky scandal, with its depositions. There is a pattern here of more than lying and coverups. It goes to the nature of people to do wrong, not just get away with an illegal activity once it is discovered and without the guilt that most of us would feel.

I. Anna and Jerry

August of 1992 was hot, no air conditioning or hot water. I was not making enough to keep up with bills and suffered from an inflamed toothache. I called the Democratic Party and left a message, offering to volunteer to do general office, phone bank or computer work. I thought I might meet some business people and get some work out of it later. Their response was positive and was on my answering machine. I found it when I got back from Jackson Hospital many weeks later.

This and a water leak to the floor below me are the two possible reasons I was taken to Jackson again where I meet Anna(Hillary's younger sister). Maybe Anna had something to do with the police and my being Baker-Acted and taken to where she worked. Basically, money was a problem and I had to charge groceries to my credit cards.

Anna was a student nurse, about thirty-two years old. I was asked to stand still by the staff when she first came up to me. Is this the First Lady candidate? Maybe, I have talked to first ladies before but she looked a little too young to be Mrs. Clinton. We get into a conversation and she seemed to be very interested in talking to me. I told her where I lived. It was not far from her and near a very good neighborhood. She asked for my phone number so I would not get into trouble. I would see her a few other times while a patient. One time she brought me some new paints, off white and a green pair. I really appreciated them and we would talk outside at times. Until a young doctor showed up, then she would run off and flirt with him. She said she was a student nurse and thinking about becoming a psychiatric nurse. She also had a beautiful English accent.

I asked for them to extract my tooth or see a dentist but not a chance, antibiotics and pain killers only.

She called me a week after I got out just like she said. So I invited her to dinner. We had to use her car. I ordered for us and as the waiter walked away, she added escargot. I complained that she did not run it by me. She said she would make it up to me. She looked just like Mrs. Clinton. So I had to order a drink from the bartender. He told me not bad and she had been in here before. We had a nice meal and conversation. She really had a beautiful personality. We went back to her place. She got in bed and looked quite receptive.

I said I had protection. She said no. I asked her if she was on the Pill. She said yes. I asked again. "Are you sure?" Her reply was that she would have an abortion before she would have my baby. I took it that she was on the Pill. The next morning I got blamed for running off one of her three beautiful cats. She feared it would not come back and it was my fault. She understood the phychology behind it.

Later Anna came by my place. She said she had heard so much about it and went though the whole place, closets and all. I stood in disbelief. I believe another time we had sex at her place. I remember a walk to the store to get a bottle of wine and we drank as the Beatles album she had taken was playing. She had wanted it, and that is enough for her to just take it. It might have been one of this administration's greatest achievements to bring back the Beatles. She was so fond of John Lennon. I told her of a poster I had seen of him and Yoko in a bookstore and she was upset I didn't get it for her. She told me I didn't have to stop smoking, but should only smoke two or three times a day like the hospital. I agreed and she said that smoking instead of work was no good. She's got a good. "Get to work." I had a computer but no car. She said on one occasion that she wanted her daughter to learn them.

One of the times I was at her place, she and some of her girlfriends came by in the morning. As she drove, I sat in the back, she was proud of me. Then they started talking in Spanish. I said Cubanos not Cubanos, I sleep with you last night. Anna started to bolt, in the car. She had a strong English accent but her Spanish was good. I immediately started worrying about some possible scheme. She said, "Wait till you meet my mother." And I better not say she is dirty. I said I was a little sorry.

Later we kidded that at least I would know what kind of automobile to get, a Trans Am. I told her that I did not mind the Cubans in Broward or the ones who wanted to be Americans first. She is probably more distant than I am.

So I was invited to Thanksgiving at her mother's house. I saw some roses and stopped. Anna liked them. I asked if we could stop and also get some wine for her mother, but she said no. When we arrived, there I gave her mother some of the roses for her hard work. There was no fighting like I was told to expect. Her brother from Disney World kept telling her when you get work do what your boss says.

She kept telling him she was going to be a nurse and that the patients seemed normal to her. Talk to Jerry. It was nice, but her sister with dark hair did seem tense at times. She finally blew up later at her girlfriend's townhouse. I never would talk like that to her very beautiful girlfriend. It was sister sister stuff I was told and they seemed proud of it.

We got to her sister's townhouse. Anna wanted a townhouse and to be with her sisters. They started that talking in Spanish. By the tone and excitement it seemed to be some type of conniving. I stayed in the kitchen. Anna came over and I grabbed a long kitchen knife and held it up. I said, "I'll let you kill me if I make a mistake." She said she would. They you better be able to finish it. She told me not to worry about that. It did get them to stop talking, then they started again.

Like Bill I don't speak Spanish but can tell when they are starting something. You can tell there is some kind of scheming going on. There were some tennis courts so I asked Anna if she would like to play. She did not know how but I talked her in to it. Her daughter came along. She stood still while I lobed them to her so she could hit them back a little. As we missed the balls Chelsea would run around and pick them up.

Chelsea really wanted her mother and me to get along. I felt sorry for her the way she ran so hard to keep us playing. Anna standing still said it was good exercise for her. Some other woman that was introduced to me as another older sister about forty took video of us playing from outside the tennis courts. She worked in New York, I was told. Anna liked everyone catering to her, with me running to return her balls. I really was touched by the way her daughter wanted Mommy and me to get along thoughout our relationship staff at Jackson told me later. I did not tell them I had gone out with Anna, how she brought her daughter by and everyone liked her. They said they would not mind raising her daughter but would not want to marry Anna. I can think of two reasons why I felt the same.

At some point, Anna told me that as a student nurse they let her look at my file. I did not care so much at the time, but it got my attention.

She called and asked if I would take her shopping for her daughter. I said yes. I had almost no concept of Christmas, I was so consumed about how to get work. Anna was on food stamps and suggested I get them. I had tried but got pushed off. Not eating was a major fact in this hospitalization, they tell me. I was eating rice three times a day. I got food stamps not long after. Maybe another reason Anna liked me she did seem to be very interested in me from the start. I didn't care very much that her sister would soon be in the White House. I did not talk politics at all with her and she was fun to be around. As I saw her more and more, she would talk about sex all the time. She had the personality of a twenty-year-old, that may of only worked a year part time. Her mother mentioned how she was going to enjoy watching "this one grow up." I was not renting like her but did not have much to offer. So I was pleased that she took to me so much and was interested in everything I did.

I was in the process of getting a car, but she took me to a possible account a few weeks out of the hospital. I was capable of work. She came in as I talked to a client about writing a custom program for his business. She told me it was hard to believe, just listening to me go over what I could do for his business with a custom program, that I had just been in a mental hospital. She made a few hints that they had picked me up just to see her or for political reasons.

She called me another time and we went to a toy store. I remember buying a chess set for her daughter and I gave her a toy car. I had several nice metal ones back at my place. I started to show Chelsea how to play chess but Mom stopped us. It was clear she did not want us to get attached, or she was just jealous.

She told me the last time or next to last time she was at my place that I should go to Michigan and live with my family. I could not understand why. She also gave me her "doctor, doctor" speech again about how she was going to marry one. She most likely knew she was pregnant at the time. In January 1993, the last time I was at her place in Hollywood, her mother was there.

The topic, to my surprise, from her mother and Anna was marriage.

I did not understand why at the time. Her mother told her I was just like her father and if that was good enough for her, it should be good enough for Anna. Again this seemed inappropriate.

Anna said I would just leave her, so why get married. Earlier she suggested we could sell my place and get a townhouse. At the time I explained that I just starting a mortgage a year ago and considered it just talk.

There seemed to be some kind of double standard that women can talk in detail about an affair but men are expected not to. I will say here we had sex twice at my place and at least once at hers. She thinks she is better than she is but if she wanted to she could do better. She was a good date though, but I had told no one that I dated her even though I had her mother's refrigerator and an old portable TV from her along with some other items. I had no intentions of getting involved in politics anymore after playing my answering machine and getting the recording of the Democratic Party calling me back with volunteer work. But they already had me in Jackson.

Anna did get me to like her and before we broke up I was having thoughts that this might be one of my last chances to have a child. She had one, that was very nice and I am so pleased to have a son. Hopefully, work will mature her and I hope we can get along, for the childrens sake. She does turn on a hate for men at times. A few months after we stopped seeing each other, the music awards were on with George Harrison. I knew how much Anna liked the Beatles and music in general, so even though it had been months, I gave her a call. She thanked me for telling her the Grammys were on and that it was okay that I called just for that.

Around that time, walking back from the store, I crossed the street near my home and there she was. Driving by, she had to slow a little as I crossed the street. Her daughter was with her. She was probably a few months pregnant with our son at the time. I thought, since she came by once after we broke up to drop off some clothes and cooking pots, that she might be waiting for her graduation from nursing school to resume a relationship. It is safe to assume that the hospital and the doctors might not have approved of her dating a patient. I was told not to even talk to other patients after I got out. Also, about that time, I looked out while at home and saw a Jag pull up across from my car. The people got out. They seemed interested in my car so I went down. They said they were with the Rose law firm. I thought, oh, lawyers or their friends. So I told them to wait, I would be right back. I came back with a few of my paintings, as lawyers in this town like to buy paintings. I set them up on my old car and talked about them for a while. They said okay and one even claimed to even understand what I meant as I described the art before they decided to leave.

I had met Mrs. Reagan and Mrs. Bush. They seemed so nice, but Hillary's family, by their own account, were a little crazy. After dating Anna and that returned call from the Democratic Party. I thought that by becoming a

Republican, it would distance me from liberals and politics.

In the early mid-1990s, back to Lock Towns after hospital. Every month, I would see a private practitioner, Dr. Glassman, on the side. Lithium is a salt and has a mild tranquilizing effect. As long as that was all I needed he would treat me and things were fine again. But Lock Town's doctors did not like me seeing other doctors. During one of my releases from the hospital, their staff tried to get me to say that I had used drugs in the last five years or ever. I assured them that all I had was a rare wine or drink. They want you to go to group therapy and to get money and keep you down and in the program. I saw a lady doctor once a month who basically just wrote a prescription. I remember she did not like something I said before I sat down and started "you're using drugs". I said you have my blood test results and you can order one anytime. Ever since I started in 1972 seeing these doctors never have any drugs been found in my system. "Well, I am a psychiatrists and I can just tell," she then wrote it down in my records. At a later visit she said wee could have gotten me out of an evaluation and treatment center where I spent nine months for writing about Jackson doctors. How much did you sue that doctor for, she asked. I started to say why and she cut me off. Just tell me! About a thousand dollars and I dropped it. She fell through her chair, quite a bit. Saying that would not even affect her mal practice insurance. During these monthly visits usually by the time you sit down they are already writing the prescriptions, for you to leave. They like to lock you, in their program and she started having met her students, do they want a private practice.

Anna kind of liked them at Lock Town, saying things like "they're hard to get away from" or "you didn't want

8

trouble from them." One time I was all dressed and literally going to the door to see my private doctor and the police knocked. I was taken to Lock Town then on to good old Jackson without seeing a doctor. I got there and used the phone after turning in my tie. The day before I had been to the beach for the first time in years. When I got out after at least a few more weeks of Jackson hospitality, I went back to see my private doctor afterwards. They said they received complaints around here. One was I was washing my car in my underwear. Actually they were my old tennis shorts that are longer than the ones you can buy now. I had a shirt on just like I ware out of here for over a year when I went to play tennis several times a week. The doctors Anna worked for believed me but jumped on it anyway as a chance to label me as a pervert. I could not understand why these doctors were against me.

There were back then even reports of me playing with myself in the shower. It got to the point that I started taking showers, in my own place, in my underwear. I live on the third floor and there is no way to see into my bathroom unless you are in my place.

In condos your property ends at the surface of the walls so you have to go through the building. One time they called H.U.D. on me because I fixed my clogged sink myself. I along with some other people who live there started using the nude beach for privacy. It took a year of going to the beach before I started using the nude beach. It was so natural there and people would talk to you. I had very few friends at the time. It seems that later talking to Anna that they were laughing how years ago I lost my shirt in business but now I have lost my pants. This was the first hospitalization after dating Anna, I had gone to the beach the day before. There I ran into two young men who laughed at my suit. When I walked away and went to up to a girl to ask for a light for a cigarette then came over to bug me. I told them if they kept it up they would be in the army by morning. The next morning I was taken to Jackson. The drivers appeared to be one of these young men. Something out of Madam X. I was wearing a business suit this time. A doctor at Jackson saw me and said he knew what this was about. I thought about Anna and at this time how she might be working there now. He told them to send me to their other mental health facility a few blocks away. For some reason the two men were very upset about this. Why they should care, I did not understand. They went with me up to the floor and talking like they were in trouble. I was perfectly okay on this hospitalization and called a lawyer just before they gave me medication.

I did not know for over a year later that I had a son from Anna. And I still do not know why it was so important to these drivers for me to go to Jackson and specifically the old section. Where Anna and I met. As of 1996, the last two times I was taken to Jackson, I had thrown an iron, water pump for my car and a mayonnaise jar out my third floor door. I wanted some press, Hillary had called and stopped an ad in the Herald. I had placed and was going to my daughters house to see her. Then I set a new covalent with my own blood on the corner of the doors. They have these Jewish symbols. And I had cleaned mine and added a cross in the entrance. May just be a new covalent there usually 2,000 years apart. I had awakened at 4:00 a.m. thinking a nuclear explosion had taken place. A dream that would not stop after, I woke up. It was some type of hero syndrome. Often when I get ill I feel if I don't do something others, or sometimes myself, will be harmed.

The medication brings me out of this. This time it was trying to get off all the excess medication I had been put on to keep me quiet about my son too fast, it brought this on. There pills can be kind of self for fullilling. I did not want to take a whole year to wean myself off, all the medication even with the help of my private doctor. So I could even read or write. That is exactly the reason for that much medication so you can't remember nor can you read and write very well. About a year later, when I stopped by to see Anna, she said she liked what I did with the iron. She didn't want to iron my shirts either.

The doctors she worked with knew I had children and wanted me down and out of circulation. They were giving me so many pills to take. Three or four maybe even five different ones several times a day each. I would drink two pots of coffee and a lot just to make breakfast. It was hard to get through the daily chores it slowed me up so much.

I don't think they cared a bit, as long as they get that perception to you and collect the money whether you end up on the street or not. They started with my not wanting me to go back to my private doctor to get on just lithium. I could and would do well on just that medicine but Lock Town and Jackson were not going to have it. I eventually joined an H.M.O. to take the authority of Jackson to have me picked up away. Otherwise, this book would never be written. They would have someone come out to see how I was doing. It was not all bad. They liked to inspect my place I complained about being overtired and could barely wash my dishes. They said, we can get you meals. How wonderful. I went to lunch once with them. It was a nice place close to where I lived. They start talking about my being on drugs to the point where the waitress asked us to leave. I could not believe it. One of them asked what do I do. I said I help young women with their investments and problems, on the beach. Then another started talking about my, going back into the hospital. Others could hear. I left and waited outside. See: Letter in Appendix Lock Town.

In late 1995, just before finding out about Shawn I started writing material for "Late Night" and was pleased that they used some of it. I had seen my son for the first time while driving by a park where Anna was walking him along the wall like she walked Chelsea when we were dating. I could not believe it and fell in love with Anna for having my baby. I also realized that he probably was the baby that Hillary was talking about adopting after the elections.

A few weeks later I decided to walk north of South Beach. The First family was in town and I had an outside chance that Anna might just be meeting with them on the Beach. Bill did run up and down Miami Beach. I knew this from a person who worked where they stay while in Miami. There is a section where English tourists go. I thought maybe Anna might be there with her accent but I did not expect it. The odds were against it but I had to try. As I walked along the shore I heard "Jerry, Jerry," and I looked up. It was Chelsea at the edge of the water. I saw Anna and Shawn on the beach.

Anna: I forgot how big your legs were and I can't take off my top. Both children held their nose and said pew pew sex. We want you as our father. I looked at my son, then back to Chelsea. Do you two get along? She replied, Yes. My son said "You got me such a nice mommy." And then he lifted his arms. "Bill is a big man. Mommy going to make me an admiral." I was shocked. Anna then says "doctor, doctor" I knew what she meant, she would have me picked up. So I started to walk away. Both children go "father, father." I stopped and turned back. My son was smiling. He looks just like Mrs. Clinton with a smile.

Anna went "doctor" again. I started to walk away. I thought of coming back but thought I could see them in a week or two at the most, so I did not double back. I still haunts me my son saying "father, father" with me walking away. I drove home in a mild state of shock and very happy. Then I started to realize. This must be the baby Mrs. Clinton wants to adopt after the elections and put in the White House for sure. I proceeded home stopping at a grocery store. The express ane was busy so I used another aisle. As I approached I saw a teenage girl looking and smiling at me. I said, "You're one of Cathy's children." As she checked out I saw her hands and face better and realized she was my daughter. She said she would wait outside. She was there with her groceries. She told me her mother just let her find me. That she decided to follow me for a while to see if she would like me as a father and that she liked having a brother related to the President. But I better talk to her mother before seeing Anna again and that they still lived on a lake and I could find the house. Anna was nice but I better check with Cathy. She would understand if I didn't. She said we could see each other on the beach. I now recognized her from the beach. She was the one who made a lot of noise once running up the walk to the lifeguard at the beach about a week earlier with her skates on. So the first time I talk to both my children was the same day. It took me a week or two to get my senses back.

I decided to try contacting my daughter's family first. They knew of my son. I knew my son was all right and I also did not want to disturb the election. Early in 1996 I decided to put my children on my income tax return. About two weeks later I got a call from Mrs. Clinton. "You put him on your tax form. You have a daughter, let us have him." Notice she never mentioned his name and no discussion. I don't remember if I had a chance to reply but she seemed upset. I have written giving them permission to have Shawn for visitations and extended stays. I received a call from Bill he was soft spoken and let me know I would be welcome to see my son in the future. It meant a lot to me to hear that but I still have not been allowed to see or talk to him once.

I had created an outline for a book titled About 80,000 Feet. About a government coverup of a pending large meteorite that, if not stopped, would destroy earth. I thought I could have lunch with some women that responded to the an ad placed and see if they could come up with some dialogue. Some women read a lot and are good conversationalists. But my effort when not.

The reason why I had placed the ad In Fan Fair a Publication of the Miami Herald it was their personals. Attractive man with love poems in one hand and tails from the bed in the Other. Please bring cut flowers. I wanted to have some fun with it. I got a call from Mrs. Clinton about two weeks later. She said she stopped my response and had all the names and numbers.

How beautiful.

I continued to go to the beach some often looking for children. I had seen a woman walking fast and she gave me the impression of being an active businesswoman. I wanted to talk to her and noticed she was talking on her cell phone so I walked past her along the shore and spotted a Navy ship just offshore. I decided to get between the ship and her. I waved my arms and she seemed pleased. It took her a while to finish talking on the phone. Finally I approached and she said that I could get my towel and sit next to her. She seemed nice and interested in talking. It was when she started talking in her little girl voice that I knew she was Madonna. We talked about children. She had watched my daughter grow up and asked me to keep writing material for "Late Night." She wanted to go and I walked her back to her car.

I liked the phone call I got the next day from Hillary explaining I was in the clear because she and Janet Reno spent an hour and a half with the photos of Madonna and me. "We never touched each other." Janet going don't get me involved in this. Janet is really a nice lady sometimes and I think they hired her because of the way she has handled me in the past. I wonder if Mrs. Clinton thought this was a chance to get something on me. Madonna had sent out a press release on us and we were all over television. Hillary and Janet Reno had to stop that press.

At Christmas 1995, I got a phone call from my daughter. She said she loved me. I had written her and her mother. I had met her years ago from some friend of a famous singer. My daughter told me she goes to places I go to and says she knows me. They tell her she doesn't know Jerry. She tell them I used to cut her mother's lawn and she was too poor to pay him I am his daughter. Not much later in January of 1996, while running my fingernails along the back left side of my scalp, I felt like a line or wire under my skin on my head. I go in with a pin underneath and then back out. It would bend the pin but I was able to break them one by one, some I cut with small wire cutters. They must have been in my head since the 1994 hospitalization were they put me under the whole weekend. I got the ones on my right side, Just as they came out my ear I counted ten. I knew they would not want this out and was scared of what they might do. I cut a piece of one off and put it in a envelope. The police were at my door and took me to Jackson within days.

They saw how well I was and knew I had just found out about my son too. I immediately asked for a writ of habeas corpus. A request for a hearing because I was being held against my will without charges. I was released without them being able to get me on the operating table again. But I was given heavy medication and had to get off of it again. I found myself getting ill from backing off all the pills too quickly but I wanted to see my children. I looked for the envelope with the short piece of wire from my head. I had saved it, but it was gone. I called Anna in June 1996. It had been at least half a year since seeing her on the beach. My son must have been about three. She said as I left a message, "I hate you, I hate you! I hate you!." This call or the next I got. I could drive by but not stop. She had Secret Service protection. I was paranoid to drive by, figured she might file some kind of stalking complaint. I drove by her mother's place once in four years and she made a big deal of it in court.

About this time I left a note on her door. Jerry and my phone number. I got a call one morning soon afterwards. Jerry. Who's Jerry? Who's he? Like I was a nothing. So I sent roses and got another call. This time she used her Cuban girl and little whore-type voice. I kept saying another girl's name, is this you. I really did not recognize her voice and thought it was some girl I had recently met on the beach. She got mad, then I recognized her voice. You got yourself a whore. I was getting calls about this time from the White House sometimes Bill or Hill and even from Janet. It was an election year.

I was very worried about all this coming out during the campaign. I suggested in writing that Anna and I were just enjoying our honeymoon while we worked out a contract marriage. I had a start on one but no feedback until I talked with her after the 1996 election. I was very happy to have a baby boy from her and did not know what else to do in order to see him.

One call I remember about this time was from Janet Reno and Mrs. Clinton. After talking to them, Bill got on and said, I want you to work with these two women, I'll be here to correct you. Mrs. Clinton started calling me. She would call when I plugged in a single line phone she said she liked it better. I usually unplugged it at night. Once she said, "Are you ready to talk?" "You are hard to get information out of." Another call, "Since you will not let us adopt your son, you're marrying my sister, that's the deal." About this time first half of 1996 she called saying she was on her way to Little Rock to lie. I watched TV and saw with in a day, her walking into court with her boots on.

In June 1996, a few weeks before July 4th, I first started hearing the news about campaign irregularities. The White House was so far ahead in the polls over Bob Dole. I bought into least some of the arguments that it all was coming from the Democratic Party probably to try and gain seats in the House and U.S. Senate. Not the presidential reelection campaign. In one of my letters I sent some jokes. If they liked them they could forward them to "Late Night." I had kept away from political jokes, but told them "No one is waving a red flag around here." A reference to foreign money for their campaign and "When are you going to invite me to the White House for family photos?" And how Hillary and Eleanor Roosevelt could go to Little Rock and look for a big stone. Later I another. People only laugh at Al Gore when he tells jokes. Bill as you can tell likes to laugh.

Mrs. Clinton started calling every morning, 8:02 a.m. she was trying to get to me. Once I would not answer. She called back in the middle of the day, all upset. So I got upset too and told her. She had to back. "No one talks to us like that." I had come right back at her every word she spoke. This is when she told me, "You got a week to get Metro under your control."

A week at four in the morning on July 4, 1996, a knock at the door. An impossible type of dilemma. They seem to know my background and that I had recently written the White House. "Have you been writing letters to the White House? This is your reply." They then said I had been Baker-Acted. I knew what was next. I was relieved when they told me I was going to a different hospital. I noticed the little handsize computers on them. I had done some programming for the trauma center and was the one to get the contract to design and program these very computers. It was part of the deal and where I was going to be compensated for my work. I finally opened the door and laid down on the floor so they could look around and then take me by ambulance.

I guess my medical records, like they said happened, changed hands at this time. This hospital's doctors knew of my struggle with Lock Towns and my complaint that they were giving me too much medicine and not letting me see a general practitioner. They were also aware of my complaint that the two doctors for years had now belittled me and were so arrogant that they dared me to just do anything but accept it. They asked an employee of Lock Town. What is this "You Hate Men" or is it the money you what your not giving him the right medication that a simple blood test reveals, he needs. In this conversation, he also said the Clintons want Anna and Jerry to get together. Why did they keep my son a secret and then away from me?

But I believe they probably did. I know Mrs. Clinton loves my son and doesn't want anything to happen to him.

In one of my letters, I suggested he and his sister spend the summers in Little Rock with them.

Then the doctors mentioned Bill was informed of this and directed a statement to a representative from Lock Towns. That it is good that Jerry and him have a sense of humor with some of this. Because you have ruined a good part of Jerry's life in the last three years. This and reference to other patients complaints as they added have my medical records. I would like to note that Lock Towns knew of my relationship with Anna and denied even her existence. Before at least one hospitalization I was calling Lock Towns and complain how can you treat me as a patient and not even tell me I have a son. I had complained to attorneys and other doctors in the 1990s that they are going to lock me up time to time no matter what I do or say. They do not like me interacting with anyone.

They locked me up twice off the same one bottle or two of wine that I still keep here. This sounds absurd but the doctors claim that a doctor and psychiatrist could tell. Explain this to my friends and clients over the years. I could continue but they asked me not to repeat this. Their representative would come to my house with other health care workers. At least this time there is a mention that the doctors are under review. I think and hope the blood tests that I asked for on them have been taken.

To give you an idea of how impossible the situation was when I was in Jackson. I believe the year 1994 after not seeing Anna for two years, I rode up the elevator with Dr. Barton, and mentioned that I had heard Anna was working in the hospital just on the other ward. This was my first experience at the new 1972 section, a much better and easier facility. He told me not to even mention that I knew her because she dates doctors now. She, with me not knowing it, had my baby and since then, the other doctors even reference in 1996 that I could be responsible for the delivery bills. But they kept it a secret that I was the father. They would not give me the name of my son either. I have found out my son's name but now I can't get them to tell me his birth date so I can get his birth certificate or the hospital or doctor that the bill came from. I repeat it was my phone calls to Lock Towns and the Miami Herald in 1996 that led to at least one of my hospitalizations. I was reporting this coverup.

I often go to the beach to see my children. On my visit to Anna, she said that I was going to the beach to try and find her.

I had seen her in a red Beetle drive by my home one morning. She went to a local high school. I parked across the street on top of a parking garage with my hood up. In a later call she said I looked like the Lone Ranger. Her boyfriend had to push start the Beetle. That is when I noticed his ponytail down to his waist. More of her John Lennon stuff. Before I got her number, I left a note simply "Jerry" and my number. I got a call the next morning.

Two weeks out of the hospital in 1996, second doctors visit weekly the new medication works well. They tell me I was not on the right medication. That the new medication would hold me, they have been right. It is some kind of appetite and sleep disorder that acts up when I worked too many hours or was under prolonged stress. They also said the Clintons would like to see Anna and me get together. I had been working in that area and allowing her to keep her personal freedom. It is what the children would like, at least some contact with me.

I started writing Anna. A few days later I got the letters back marked "return to sender." One contained a small check. I sent some more roses and love to her and her children. She accepted. I want my son to know his father, thinks of him. In 1995, the last time I saw him, he said "father, father" as I walked away and Anna's "doctor, doctor" scared me.

I got Anna's phone the first time I called and got a man. I explained I had no romantic interest in Anna. But she did have my son and I wanted to see him. He seemed to accept that. The second time, I call and get denial, from a young man, then after explaining I had a lawyer verify the number this week. He said, "You know what I could do to him (Shawn)." A threat to harm my son if I did not leave them alone.

I called the *Miami Herald* news desk. They said they would have a reporter get back to me. I called Anna back to let them know and to reduce the chance of my son being molested. And that both Clintons suggested that I try and talk to her.

In August 1996, I called Anna and left a message to please call and discuss a visitation agreement, so I wouldn't need to spend money on attorneys, I would rather send it to her. In September 1996, I tried to call and got Anna's answering machine. She used her "normal" voice, her Anna voice as she referred to it, vis Soljo a slang name she uses.

About September 17, 1996, I called the Miami Herald again on the local news desk was Jone Flashman. She heard the short version of my story and attempt for visitation rights. She said to notify her when an attorney filed. I relayed this to counsel.

She was pleased with the news that a reporter had been contacted. She said the Larry King show would probably be interested in having us on. Kidding. You have to consider just that Hillary has a sister that looks just like her and has been kept a secret all this time is a story.

I called Anna on impulse because I had just updated this. She told me that she called the police already and Jackson and her husband, she had to stop from killing me. I got in that there was something important. If I file in court for visitation then the press will be in on this and that I had wrote Bill and Hillary about this. I got in that child support from me is one of her rights, as visitation is one, of mine. She hung up.

But this shows how a history of a neurological based disorder triggerred by excess work, stress or alcohol at times can be used as a tool to get the other party's way. I did say in this conversation that Jackson and its doctor at Lock Towns where she had studied and worked around are not to be used, as henchmen.

In late 1996, I would call Anna's mother. She was reasonable at times, even kidded me about how now I was mixed with her family. She asked me if the box I had sent was toys. I said yes and she told me to send them to her. I was so happy to do so. I resent them to her but they came back again "return to sender." Now I knew the only answer was court.

The changing of her phone number and her refusal to accept my mail left me only the Clintons to write to. They had given me called me before and they seemed okay but it was their, points that came across with never a discussion.

In 1996, before the hearing I called Anna's mother on the weekend. Sometimes her mother had a sense of humor. She liked me and would kid about what it was like to be tied to her daughters.

In January 1997, we went to court for child visitation and support. Under oath both Anna and her mother claimed Anna never gave birth to a male child. The newspaper ran an article that showed I did have a relationship with Anna, but no Shawn. Devastated and scared a little by their blatant lying, I continued to see a psychiatrist as required, avoiding the topic of Shawn. I asked about people that lie all the time and don't care if it causes damage. Some of them feel the world owes them.

They don't feel guilty and often go on to do illegal things. Is there any medication for this? The answer was no and if there was they could empty the prisons. Finally on a visit I mentioned my son.

I got an immediate response that there was a coverup and I better not even say I have a son, or else they would kill me on the operating table. It was not until another six months passed and the lying in the Paula Jones case concerning Monica occurred that I saw hope. (See letter in appendix to F.B.I. concerning this death threat by Dr. Sabas.)

On Fathers Day 1997, I send roses to Mrs. Clinton's mother thanking her for taking care of Shawn. I wanted my son to know he had a father. I also called the Secret Service and the White House to ask if I could see my son for an hour before Fathers Day. They thought it was a reasonable request but no response.

On December 3, 1997, I went to court in Broward refile but I did not have enough in writing. Just an impressive list of numbers to call besides doctors. The aid commented, "I did not even know she had a sister." As I explained, he stated. "This is a coverup." Several times.

On Christmas Eve 1997, I called Anna's mother to wish her and her family a happy Christmas. I told her I would like to send flowers and asked if she could tell Shawn I love him. She said there was no little boy named Shawn and she would just have to refuse the flowers. Then she said we might get her one of those places, a reference to a townhouse and maybe I need to save my money for it. She said, now I would rather see Anna live with me then there would be something other than gay orgies, and by her tone she wished things were different. I told her the F.B.I. knew there was a boy. She said no F.B.I. in the world knew there is a Shawn. So I told her I wished the best. Perhaps I can get used to the lying all the time. Their lying has gotten them this far so why not just stick to it. She was nice to me in person and a mental patient is the best Anna can do, it sounds like a good match. I feel like their therapist. I could tell from the first time I met Mrs. Clinton's mother that she worked but her family was what was most important. It would be an improvement if Anna and Hillary were more like her.

Just before the end of the 1998 election, I wrote the White House asking for Shawn's birth date as a sign they would at some point work with me. But no response, so I called one of their attorneys in Washington, Mr. Bennett, and asked, if he would run it by them. I had to call back after the election. I got from his office that I was a schizophrenic and that Hillary did not even have a sister. So I told them I would write until I die.

I tried calling twice in 1998 after Monica and the perjury story broke. But Hillary's mother was just too upset. I felt good that after a year of living with the results of Anna and her mother's perjury that someone was getting it for lying in court. Finally I called on Christmas Day apparently getting one of Anna's girlfriends. She seemed nice. I asked for permission to send some toys but she could not okay it.

February 4, 1999, was one of my usual visits to Dr. Weingrod, except I had mailed her a copy of the restraining order Anna had on me. She had indicated that she wanted to see it because she thought Anna was going too far. So I started talking about it and how I could get an attorney but it would be pretty expensive. And I brought up my book about the Clinton's and how that could pay for court. She said she thought I needed to go into a hospital. I disagreed, saying I have felt the same for years now and am doing well on the medication. So when I got home I called the Republican Party and told them I was being hospitalized for what I thought were political reasons. I also called my general practitioner and asked to make arrangements for a blood test, even though I had just had a physical so they could check my brain chemistry. I also asked her to call Dr. Weingrod and have her stop the hospitalization. I had made a tape recording of the visit with the doctor and said the recording would speak for itself as to the real reason I was being Baker-Acted. Then I decided to call Dr. Weingrod's office myself and see if I could talk her out it. Her secretary said she didn't like the way I had left and asked if I could come right back. I said I could be there in twenty minutes and that's why I wanted to talk to her. I hid my tape and then returned to the doctor's office with a copy of my manuscript on computer disk to give her. I saw a police car but went in anyway. They had told the police I had treatened to physically harm them and they restated that in front of me. I told the police I had made no such statement and asked to file a police report of my own.

I claimed she had made a false police report. I gave the police the diskette of this book for the doctor. He took it and gave it to her. The police were understanding but transported me to the hospital. I was interviewed several times and asked about threatening the doctor. I told the truth and a few days later, one of the doctors at the hospital told me they had talked to Dr. Weingrod and she had said I had not threatened her. But what was the real reason I was hospitalized? She thought my medication needed to be adjusted? No. Your book about Clinton. He told me some time they turn over to the Secret Service people talk talk about the Clintons. I said that was okay. In the 1980s I did some computer work for two different businesses whose owners had relatives with the Secret Service and they had found me.

I had recognized some people at this mental hospital who had worked at Jackson in the early 1990s and they knew Anna from work. I told them how I had gone out with her and kept it a secret and then she kept my son a secret. They said it's a secret. I also enjoyed using my sister Hillary as the relative they should contact in case of an emergency and giving them the name of my son and Anna as a relative for the hospital records.

In May 1999, since it was Anna's birthday and Mothers Day, I thought I might try some roses it had been a long time. I got a call a day or two later in the afternoon from a young man saying he was with my daughter, the one I was looking for. I said I have a daughter. Then he said, "Yea, your daughter Shawn. Right now." He said, "I better leave these people alone because I am with your daughter now." I don't want to continue but I called the police and the authorities to check on my son.

It has been over thirty days and Florida State HRS was to give me a report as to my sons condition. But I was told they reached the conclusion that there is no Shawn. I gave them information in writing and told them I have additional evidence if that was not enough because I know Anna could, as she did simply claim she does not have a son.

During this time the F.B.I. stopped by my fathers house and told him they know I have a son. He asked them if they were sure and their response it would take a DNA test to proof. They also asked him what he knew about the implants in my head and that they knew I had been writing the White House. The Secret Service had visited me back on April 30, 1999, and told me they had received complaint about my internet site www.couceiro.com and letters to the White House. I have written the Clintons every month for over three years letting them know I am interested in my son and giving them the business a little along with the truth.

They believed the real reason they were upset is me reporting Anna selling cocaine to the physiatrist. With the F.B.I. and them giving me credit I would like to accept. Anna told me the Clintons said if some thing came of it they would get me. They claim my writing is treating but a review of their complaint cleared me. I also signed a medical release of my records so the Secret Service could check out my claim of implaints in both ears. Now I have received a request from Anna mother she wants a restraining order on me. She filed with the court that I think I have a son from her daughter. The denial and lies continue.

II. Thanksgiving 1996

I had stopped by the Hollywood Police before going to Anna's. I figured she would throw some kind of fit as she apparently had something to do with several of my hospitalizations and took credit for being with the C.I.A.. It could be the same brain disorder her sister had. I had found out my son's name from a day care center where she had taken his sister too. When I dated her back in 1992, I had a camera just in case I saw my son. The neighbor had told me a few days earlier that he had never seen a boy ever and that she had a daughter and dog. Also Anna was in and out a lot but he had a wife. The day care center talked of her other sister, a dark-haired short woman who would be with her when she picked up the children.

I arrived and parked my car across from her property. I knocked and said "Anna, it is Jerry." She said Jerry, Jerry, I haven't seen you. I want to see you. Come here, I want to see you. Shouldn't you be in a mental hospital? I think you should be in a hospital. Her daughter opened the door. It's Jerry. Is Shawn here? No. I miss him, I wish you and mommy would quit fighting. Anna came out. I want to see what you look like so I can tell what my son will look like. Me and my mother have a problem with our noses (sure like Pinocchio). The doctors at Broward hospital won't go out with me. I wanted a girl because of your nose, lips and eyes. What did you come here for? Usually people come here for sex. I see your car, it is a big car. Is this what you waited for? (a reference to my waiting an additional month to get a car when we were dating). What do you want? You don't have a son. I said I had seen him at the beach. She got upset. Had it not been for that we could have pulled it off. Bill is a better man than you. I hear you were in the hospital again. Notice how they keep bringing you to me. When are you going to stop? I called there and they said you were there for masturbating too much. I laughed. Then I told them I knew what to do with that. What I like about you is the money comes in even if you are in the hospital. Shouldn't you be in a hospital? I think you should be in a hospital.

Look at me. I want to see my son Shawn. How did you find that out his name and my phone number? I saw him and you and his sister on the beach. We had him adopted and you can't find him, was her reply. He came out nice. I would not mind having another. I want a big family. He is going to be someone. You sure got us back with Madonna. Do you want to stop? To see if we can get along? A suntan all over your body excites me. You are sending personal information to the White House. They will get you if something comes of this. I can't stop you. Put it in your book and watch what happens.

Your son starts with wanting his father. Then my daughter starts. I don't know why she took to you so much. But you would make a good father for her. I have to do something. If you don't work this out in private I am going to take you to court. You over here on the weekends and you're a writer. Yes. At this point I should have given in a little bit. She likes it if you give some extra besides being fair.

Then she started to laugh. Well, Jerry it has been about five years now. You should have enough in your place for a townhouse. We will sell it and get a townhouse. That's what I want. There is no privacy there. I want a townhouse and your furniture. We could get married, and I would have time to figure a way to kill you. What I like about this when we get through fighting no one will mess with us. Writing for Dave of "Late Night" was cool. I know you can be cool. Remember I told you to suck on my small tit to make it bigger. Well, you didn't. So I had your son and now you have made it like the other. Remember that I will always find a way to get you to do what I want. You suck, don't worry you will get to suck me again. I like the way you suck.

I let them watch "Star Trek", I saw in your medical records that you figured out how those things work. I figure you must be smart. I wanted a girl but I tell your son his father is Data. Watch they keep taking parts of his brains in and out. I like how you think Shawn would be good for my daughter.

I had left a note a few days earlier when she was not in. How about the hundred thousand. Maybe. Then I won't have to work. I am the mother! I'll give him, to you! I can have another! Then the police she had called came. I haven't stopped by here in four years to see Anna. It has been over a year since I saw my son. That was all I am here for. She carried on about my illness and how in my mind this seems real. I told the police how many years I had known the doctors that she worked for and how I found out my son's name at the day care and the three women remembered him. Now I would just go to court. The policeman told me don't say anymore and I'll let you leave. He checked my coat for a weapon. This is how you, should dress if you come here. If I see you again, I will throw you, in prison.

The officer. Lady if there is a son. I am a RN. I patrol this area lady you're no nurse. He then had her tell me I am trespassing on private property. Then, her last remark as I left. That wasn't bad.

III. Visitation and Child Support

January 1997, Jerry Kletke vs. Anna Couceiro, CASE# 96-015756, asking for visitation and child support. Waiting outside the court in the morning, Anna and her mother arrive with her daughter Chelsea.

She sees I brought a cooking pot she gave me. Her reaction as she walked by. This is what you get when you try and help people! It seemed that she has an oh so appropriate little green shirt on. They went to the room just outside the hearing room. I waited outside then took a seat where I could see her as the door opened and closed. She smiled. Later she drew attention to her daughter, on the floor playing.

I thought of how she and my son must play together. A man came out later saying there was a woman with a child. She says her daughter has a high temperature and they should go next. That's Anna. I thought I would go to the door and see if she would speak to me. A security man that came in with them said no. Later, after we were inside. He would state, you took it out. I told them they could not get away with saying I had no contact with them.

We got to go in I sat across with the Broward Sun-Sentinel next to me with a photographer. Mrs. Clinton's mother, Anna and her daughter were across. They noted the presence of the Sun newspaper and the judge announced a federal observer. Anna kept hiding her face. She looked at me. Then the cameraman started, they had already taken pictures of me. She looked at me "real good." I am sure she liked the reporter, too.

Judge Greene said he knew this case was coming for two weeks and felt like a federal judge. Then I heard about the Paula Jones claim. We got acquainted, I mention, if the judge had one of these a reference to local women. He said no. He told me he did not like my tan. I took it seriously and slightly uncertain. He then mentioned to Anna how she really gets around but that was okay you're in intelligence. Her response, "That's right." And he thinks he's in it and he cannot even speak Spanish. He should be on more medication, in his mind this is real.

There is the pot where is the plant and you got your F.B.I. cowlick going. Judge to Anna. You will say anything. The judge made a reference that he understands that it was hard for me to get a witness or attorney to sit next to me.

The judge asked me to read the claim, which I did. Upon the pronouncing of their last name, I was stopped by Anna and my pronouncing was corrected. I said that I never had heard you or any member of your family use it. She laughed and the judge said very good.

Her mother said to me softly she liked the idea of me helping her daughter (Anna) into a townhouse. She had brought my letter and mentioned how I gave her some roses that I picked up with Anna at Thanksgiving.

You're going to end up with everything. Looking at my evidence. They stated to the court in writing that they had only seen me in the hospital for a short time four years ago. There was a letter they had written to the court. I was told by the judge that it was sent, but have not seen it yet. The judge was brief and interested in expediting the process.

After we were sworn in, I mentioned Thanksgiving dinner then Anna's mother admitted they had me over for Thanksgiving dinner. She commented she never thought she would see her pot again. I said so you recant what you put in writing to me and this court. Would you like to continue. The answer was no. I said there are some other things in there that are pretty good. Then the judge stepped in and said having Thanksgiving dinner with you is no small matter! I take it he did not like them lying. (They had apparently also made a case to him that I belonged in a mental hospital.) I looked at Anna's mother and said I did not need everything now.

The judge wanted to move this along. I have a couple of questions and since you're under oath and they're important. The judge asked are either of you related to Mrs. Clinton. Both answered "no". The judge was taken back. I can just see Mrs. Clinton sitting right between you two. Let's try this one.

Excluding any abortions to Anna and her mother I want you to answer this too. Did you ever give birth to a male child? Both said. "no". He said he happened to know there was a boy. The judge asked if I had any more evidence and if I had an attorney, I could win this. He did not let me go over all my written evidence but said I could give it to him and that he would read it later. Tell me how you know you have a son? The first time, I saw him, I had driven by a park, I recognized Anna's car and she was walking my son on the wall as we had done a few years earlier with her daughter. His legs and shape of his head were like me, I had a very strong emotional response.

A few weeks went by. I decide to go to South Beach to look. As I walked along the beach, Anna's daughter was by the edge of the water she said "Jerry, Jerry, it's Jerry." I looked to the left and saw Anna and my son. He was so happy, sitting there. Anna said I forgot how large you legs are. I asked both of her children if they got along and they said yes. My son lifted his arms and goes Bill is a big man and he motioned with his hands. Then mommy going to make me an admiral. The judge said, okay, stop. Who would not want that.

Anna went as I lifted my hands like Shawn did said he is just like his son what do I need him for. Why don't you let Bill have him, he ran all the way down the beach to see him! Judge Greene said he had listened to phone calls but he could not listen to the ones from the White House. Could I tell him so he could decide? I asked which one. The first. I told him the first from Bill was business. Anna said business if he knew anything about business he would be rich. The judge asked about another. Bill said once my son would be a football player and I could visit and play with him out in Arkansas. Then one from Hillary where she claimed the TV I threw out was hers and not to throw anymore of their stuff out. I was interrupted by Anna saying she gave me that TV and the judge said what did you do for them? If I had thier TV I would feel like a federal judge and fix it.

Then the judge said that, he would allow me to refile and that I should ask for him to hear the case. I felt despair that some kind of settlement would not be reached here. Said that he had some problems with me. He early on let us both know that he was well read about our history. I can't count the lies, I have been told by Anna and her mother through this. I have reached the conclusion that it is psychopatic-type lying. It is clear that they get some kind of pleasure from being able to get what they want by lying. Anna mentioned they got the $20.00 check, I had looked for it and knew it had been taken out of my place. It was to her and she signed the back of it, proof. I had looked for it as evidence of a relationship out of the hospital. Copies of legal document and tapes were also missing. I had concluded they were taken by Dr. Matista of Lock Town, their people that admitted to going completely through my place more than once. At this point I was excited, and the judge said I better calm down. He asked if I was like this with my daughter's mother. I said there was nothing between my daughter and me. Anna said I like his daughter Mariah Carey but I don't like him. Judge said to Anna, you like her money. (I have a daughter but she is not M. Carey.) He asked about the 1980s and other children. (I didn't feel comfortable answering at that time. So I smiled, Anna goes he a little whore like me, they don't need to know about are sex in the 1980s. The judge I can see you been around attorneys. I know I am the father.

Then they started asking for a restraining order. After her mothers third reason before I could respond to the first. Anna was talking too. So I turned to her when she mentioned that I sent roses. The judge said roses are harassment and the two letters and toys were refused. Anna looked right at me and said head on. The judge said, Oh they're going to have sex right here. Now, their in love with each other.

Anna's mother was still going with her complaints. I stopped and said go ahead. I don't care if I have a restraining order from them. Judge Greene, you don't. I only went to their place once in four years. They looked shocked and disappointed. It had become a game to call them. Even though I kept it to the weekends. The judge granted it but said I am sure he is not dangerous. The judge knew that I was well watched and on top of that they have federal security, Secret Service.

If he breaks it (the order) I'll send him to jail then over to you at Broward General that would be fine. Judge I would like to stop that. She then says, he is really very sweet. Then I started moving the large pot around. There something in here. It got quiet. I looked at Anna and said if I had my son's birth date then I would be over for you. She just looked. I opened the pot. And like Marsha Clark said, look what we got here. It was some clothes. The judge noticed one was purple (from India by the way). Anna said Oh my God. Then the judge I'll give you there was some sex. Like Marshs Clark and you are going to lose this.

The judge asked me to give a closing argument. Anna looked shocked. Then after a second I held out my hands (like that defense attorney). The judge had said believe me he is winning this. Ready to ask the question. What to do with two birds, in my hand. The judge stopped me and said he would handle that. I asked if there would be a gag order, if I ask for a delay his response, you can bet on it.

I gave the judge my Dave, Mrs. Clinton's stare. Anna goes that's it. It is my sister that loves him. The rest of us hates him and I hope he sleeps with her. Then Bill will kill him. Then I will be done with him and get a little something. The judge said this is like the second family here and are they into sex!

He then ruled I did not present enough evidence. How beautiful goes Anna. I will get you a pretty girl. I stood up slowly and then ask the court to be seated. Saying I'll have to come up with a work around. Anna's response. He is a nut.

Anna says now all I got is federal trafficking to worry about. The judge said that's a beautiful way to make a living and you will not even let him see his son at all. I did not leave all but I left some windows for you. She said that's okay, then I have something he wants.

Talking to I. Couceiro. First, and say to the bailiff to have me leave. The judge told Mrs. Clinton's mother something better have not happened to the boy. Then why are you doing this? Weeks before: This hearing, The Court had done a discovery, but still told me I would needed a birth certificate. I thought, it would come through since now I had my son's name. But vital statistics asked for the exact birth date too. As I left Anna said I hope your computer breaks. She stated again, there must be something wrong with the checks and balances again. I talked to the reporter outside. He said he follows Mrs. Clinton's mother for his paper (Henry Fitzgerald). And asked why I would want to have to pay child support. I didn't respond but stated they lied in there, people do lye.

IV. Foreign Funds

The Federal Bureau of Investigation through electronic surveillance and other counterintelligence measures directed at the Chinese Embassy in Washington discovered that the Beijing government planned to influence the 1996 presidential elections through donations to the Democratic National Committee. In response, the Justice Department ordered twenty-five investigators to the counterintelligence operations and notified members of Congress.

Webster Hubbell was not a major player in the campaign scandal but received money from one of its players. Webb Hubbell had just pleaded guilty to illegal activities such as tax evasion and mail fraud. That occurred when he was with the Rose law firm and he ended up spending eighteen months in a Maryland prison. He was down financially when he received work from John Huang of Lippo. A week before Hubbell received this payment of $100,000, Haung of Lippo Banking, both friends of Clinton from Little Rock, visited the White House. About the same time Commerce Secretary Ron Brown helped Lippo get a dam project in China.

He also received a total of $750,000 from a collection of Clinton supporters, many visitors to White House coffees or sleepover guests in the Lincoln bedroom. Hubbell had a bad memory during the Whitewater hearings and trial. Starr granted him immunity to testify to other matters and it got worse.

In November 1998, Starr brought fifteen new indictments against Hubbell and some involved his relationship with Mrs. Clinton and the failed Whitewater land deal that they both worked on. Hubbell had said in testimony that Hillary had little to do with the dealings but billing records showed up two years after they were requested in the White House residence right after Hubbell testified. The record shows Hillary did have a significant role. The charges included perjury, fraud, and false statements interfering with the function of the Federal Deposit Insurance Corp. The insider land deal had fictitious sales and land flips. The indictments claim Hubbell covered up and concealed the true nature of the land development, with Hillary having a role, at the Rose law firm where they both worked. Foster also worked at the Rose law firm; he and Hubbell both came to Washington with the Clintons. It is believed Foster had possession of the billing records at that time. Their close friends the McDougals, also were involved and the failure. Mr. McDougal died in jail after being convicted of these matters. And his wife, Susan, also served time. Anna told me in 1996 that she met the McDougals when they were in such trouble over this and that they were nice people.

A reference to how they are in trouble. Everything for "it" Hillary was her explanation. I found she likes to be nice to people herself and then demand they do illegal things for her. I said no to an illegal idea of hers, then she really got upset.

Sleep Overs and Coffees:

There were 102 coffees at the White House during the 1996 election. J. Huang is reported to have made a speech that included the following, "Elections, as you know, cost money, lots of money and I'm sure everyone in this room will want to support the reelection of the President."

As a DNC fund raiser Charles Trie also arranged and brought Wang Jun, who worked for a Chinese military weapons trading company, to one of many now famous White House coffees with Clinton during the 1996 reelection campaign. Clinton now says he should not have met with Wang. Trie also delivered $640,000 for the President's legal defense fund. This money has also been returned.

J. Chung brought six businessmen from China to hear Bill deliver a short speech and have a photo opportunity with them in the Oval Office. He delivered $50,000 that day and since 1994 $366,000 was paid to the DNC.

Just Friends from Arkansas:

Johnny Chung was born in Taiwan and became an engineer. After viewing a debate between Bush and Clinton in 1992, he said he just went to the Governor's mansion in Little Rock and knocked on the door where he met Hillary. This became a long-time friendship with both Clintons.

John Huang is registered as Vice-Chairman and acting president of Lippo Bank. The Riadys from China founded the bank. Mochtar Riady is a financier and also a frequent visitor of the Clinton White House. The bank is located in the Chinatown district of Los Angeles and has had bad real estate loans.

Banking regulators are scrutinizing many transactions just under $10,000 and totaling 7 million from accounts to the Riady Bank in Hong Kong. Ken Quincy who had over site of the bank for the FDIC, and Huang of the Commerce Department had phone calls and White House visits that coincided.

J. Chung fled the country to avoid a subpoena like almost a hundred others who either left the county, which in itself is a crime, or took the Fifth Amendment. But J.

Chung returned in March to face charges of bank fraud and tax evasion. Cooperating with investigators, Chung told how he ran $100,000 into the White House through Liu Huaqing's daughter who is now a top military commander in China. These are China military and Chinese party members. This is accepting money from a foreign government, which is in conflict with campaign laws. If it is hard money (used directly by the candidate), it is also unprecedented. At the end of the reelection in 1996, as these allegation, surfaced, Bill Clinton said it was all over in the DNC. But Louis Freeh, director of the F.B.I., said he did not notify the White House of the Chinese funding of the elections because he believed they were involved.

J. Chung has also stated to investigators that Lt. Colonel L. Chaoying gave $300,000 to be delivered to the Democrats. He also routinely gave small amounts to "straw donors" as reimbursement for their individual donations. It is illegal to donate money for a second party. He has been indicted for doing the same for Democratic Senator John Kerry who became the U.S. Ambassador to China during the Clinton Administration. You probably will not find any direct quid pro quo on paper but the money got results. It was disclosed in April 1999 by J. Chung that the Clinton reelection campaign took $300,000 from General Ji Shenglde, chief of China's military intelligence. It is reported that the general said, "We like your president." J. Chung said he was introduced through Liu Chaoying, the daughter of a retired general and a lieutenant colonel in China's People's Liberation Army.

Charley Trie:

Dan Burton, House Committee: Discloses investigations that show C. Trie gave Foung and Landon $35,000 to pass to DNC and $5,000 to J. Huang for donations. Charles Yah Lin Trie owned a restaurant that Bill used to frequent when he was governor. He gave $639,000 to Bill Clinton's Defense Fund in the Whitewater case. It was returned for being of questionable origin. His restaurant received a $60,000 loan from the Lippo group, as he is a friend of J. Huang. He also donated more than $200,000 to the DNC. He visited the White House at least twenty-three times. He also accompanied a Chinese arms dealer into a White House coffee. Later Bill said he should not have had him in the White House.

Trie: Developed a friend Mr. Wu described as a business advisor to the Chinese Government and Communist Party. Arlen Specter said this virtually makes him a Chinese government official. Wu himself is involved in donations through other parties where he would reimburse donors for their contributions. Bank records reveal Trie received $905,000 from Mr. Wu. On January 28, 1998, Charlie Trie was indicted by a federal grand jury. But Trie had fled the country.

President Clinton picked James Wood from Arkansas for the American Institute in Taiwan in 1995. He was accused of soliciting foreign funds for Bill Clinton's reelection by the Justice Department and stepped down from his post on January 17, 1997. James Wood also visited China with J. Huang.

Thompson Hearings:

The hearings produced indictments against Charlie Trie and Maria Hsia and charges against Johnny Chung and Yogesh Grandhi for fund raising efforts.

John Glenn said the hearings had a potential to be a catalyst for public uproar. But that did not happen and no legislation resulted. If all we get is the existence of illegal allegations and no more, it will be a loss.

It was disclosed that, during the period of October 1994 through November 1995, J. Huang received thirty-seven secret briefings and was given reports that were kept in a safe, from the C.I.A.. Others at Commerce attended the meetings and the reports were said to be business and investment information on Asia. The C.I.A., questioned at the Thompson hearing, said they were not aware of J. Huang ties with Lippo including phone calls or his visits to the Chinese Embassy in Washington.

Perjury:

Thompson was asked if anyone lied. He replied "Sure" with the ones that he has documentary evidence on will be referred to the Justice Department. Senator Thompson referenced Watergate and how Nixon had instructed people just to say then, "I do not remember."

Rap Up:

Thompson said if Justice had been more aggressive and a grand jury was running simultaneously, they could have been more effective but he takes credit for pushing Janet Reno into bringing on board some real good investigators and renewed his call for an independent council to be set up. As these hearings closed a new panel was being set up in the House by Dan Burton and has no time limit. He asked Lott for an extension of the public hearings, but weakness even among some Republicans prevented it. The President declined to testify voluntarily.

Dan Burton House:

J. Chung is quoted as referring to the White House as a subway. "You have to put the coins in to open the gates." Apparently he likes doing business with the American Government and now is in deep water. J. Chung asked for and got a letter from Don Fowler, Chairman of the DNC, introducing him from the White House for his upcoming trip to China. Was it something to show the boys from China a job well done? It is illegal to make a donation in someone else's name, but according to J. Chung's friends, that is exactly what happened. They told investigators that J. Chung would reimburse them immediately for $1,000 donations to the Clinton Gore reelection campaign.

On November 13, 1997, the First Lady's Chief of Staff, Maggie Williams, testified to accepting a $50,000 check from J. Chung. Accepting a donation on White House property is a federal violation of campaign laws and so is accepting foreign money. Williams told how J. Chung was a frequent visitor of the First Lady's office and he really admired her. The Secret Service records show J. Chung accessed the White House at least forty-nine times on a pass from Hillary's office.

Democrat Henry Waxman had a sense of humor. He calls the more than fifty visits to the White House and hundreds of thousands of dollars from J. Chung no big matter by Washington standards. J. Chung attended numerous functions like coffees, parties, movies and a radio address, but then no policy favors ever ensued from this.

On November 14, 1997, J. Chung was to take the Fifth, if put under oath, but he agreed to talk behind closed doors after they threatened to put him on TV taking the Fifth in the hearing. He should be able to shed light on these investigations.

On March 6, 1998, Johnny Chung agreed to cooperate with the Justice Department in the 1996 campaign Democratic fund raising scandals. The November 1998 sentencing of J. Chung by Federal Judge Real was delayed due to a inappropriate letter from the Democratic National

Committee. Attorneys on each side objected in open court and the judge invoked a delay until the matter could be resolved. J. Chung faces thirty-seven years and a $1.45 million fine for his role in illegal campaign donations to the reelection of Al Gore and Bill Clinton in 1996 as well as bank fraud and tax evasion. He is alleged to have contributed illegally to Senator John Kerry of Massachusetts, a Democrat and current ambassador to China. J. Chung pleaded guilty back in March 1998 to the reelection money. Sentencing was rescheduled for November 16, it came down on the November 14, 1998. It is a criminal offense to try and influence a judge in a case. The DNC doesn't need any more attention to this matter. The letter disputes J. Chung's claim that the DNC solicited the contributions.

Part of Campaign Financing Task Force:

J. Chung is given five years' probation. He had pleaded guilty to bank fraud, tax evasion and making illegal political donations to the 1996 campaign. Brain Sun told of his cooperation with the government that is investigating illegal contributions. Prosecution agreed with the sentence, given Chung's cooperation with the two year investigation.

On August 27, 1998, Dan Burton, acting as chairman of the Government Reform and Oversight, looked into campaign abuse. They called Huang and Webster Hubbell to testify and produce documents in reference to fund raising. They both took the Fifth Amendment.

Burton writes, in response to Janet Reno's refusal to honor a committee's subpoena for specific documents regarding possible abuse of campaign regulation, that the Justice Department had stated it lacked precedent.

The letter opens:

Dear Attorney General Reno:

On December 8th 1997, you made the following statement:

It is unprecedented for a congressional committee to demand internal decision making memoranda generated during an ongoing criminal investigation.

Although this statement was clearly a misrepresentation of fact, I initially dismissed it as political posturing. More recently, however, you and your spokesmen have repeated the substance of this statement, and I have become concerned that you and your staff have embarked on a conscious decision to mislead Congress and the American people.

He continues by saying it is becoming obvious that she is protecting the President, Vice President and congressional members from another independent counsel. And how L. Freeh the FBI director, and La Bella concurred the memorandum should be sent. And La Bella, head of the task force said it demands the appointment of an independent counsel. L. Freeh said at the close of the 1996 campaign he did not inform the White House of the investigation of illegal foreign campaign money coming in because he believed some was from the White House itself.

Trent Lott stated publicly that we do not need another ninety-day review period but that is what we got. In October 1998, Dan Burton asked the Federal Election Commission to investigate $600,000 that he considers clearly illegal and another about $1.2 million in possibly illegal contributions. This money has not been returned like most other questionable contributions. He also pointed out they now have the connection to the Riady family's

Lippo group for the $45,000 received from the Buddhist Temple the day before Al Gore arrived. It was a check to reimburse donors for their $15,000 each donation. More money laundering. Al Gore has now admitted he knew it was going to be a fund raising event arranged by the DNC and his Chief of Staff. On November 8 1998, a grand jury returned indictments for illegal donations in 1992 to the Clinton-Gore 1996 campaign. Illegal donations began in 1992, the Clinton for President committee and ended in 1995. Indictments accepted by U.S. District Court by Judge Alan Kay. Franklin L. Haney of Chattanooga, Tennessee, faces forty-four counts. He is alleged to having made illegal contributions. He is a real estate developer, who donated a million dollars in the form of a fee to Peter Knight, Clinton's campaign manager at the time and appointed by Clinton to be ambassador to China. Former Senator James Kerry from Massachusetts may also have received donations. GOP-House Commerce Committee's investigation looked into reports and asked the Justice Department to investigate the matter.

Al Gore Accepts Money:

Al Gore's role in questionable money raising seemed to be limited to the Hsi Lai Temple visit in 1996. He has denied knowing the event was a fund raiser as it is illegal for nonprofit religious and foreign campaign money to be contributed to American elections. John Huang of the DNC arranged the fund raiser on April 29, 1996, outside of Los Angeles, California. It was a $2,500 per person luncheon.

Three Buddhist nuns are granted immunity just before the House hearing. They claim in testimony that $45,000 was donated to the DNC the day before the Al Gore visit and an additional $55,000 raised the day after his address and $65,000 of $100,000 was laundered by the Temple. Temple members were being reimbursed for their donations. Is there a qui pro quo working here with Taiwan? The nuns, under questioning, said they had done this before for Patrick and Ted Kennedy. The committee felt they proved the temple had acted as a "conduit" back in 1992 and 1993. And a total of $113,000 in illegal donations are now accounted for. Senator Thompson requested the video that was made of the fund raising luncheon.

Gore's denial is hard to believe. As Republican senators point out, Gore's own records kept by the Bill Clinton and Al Gore reelection campaign show their projections of $200,000 for the luncheon. His staff refers to it as a fund raiser. This engagement was arranged by this same staff.

Yi Chu, a Temple administrator, testifies before a Senate committee in September 1997, that he tried to raise an additional $100,000 for Washington by asking his members to give $5,000 each. John Glenn, sitting on the panel, asked Yi Chu if any of the money came from foreign sources. His response was denial, "Not at all." A nun testifying said she discarded the list of donors that contributed to the $45,000. To avoid causing embarrassment to the Temple was the reason given. And she destroyed some of the other Temple's accounting records and documents. The DNC returned $140,000 in funds from what they refer to as a community event, not an official fund raiser. Al Gore finally admitted it was a mistake to attend the event. This prompted Republicans to ask Janet Reno to appoint an independent counsel to look into Asian business money coming and the Clinton-Gore presidential election efforts. Two other players, Huang and Hsia, took the Fifth Amendment and are refusing to testify in this matter. On September 5, 1997, e-mail evidence showed that Al Gore himself referred to the Temple visit as a fund raiser. David Strauss, Al Gore's chief of staff, testified. Strauss had claimed Gore knew nothing about the fund raising nature of the event. Gore did not testify. Soft/Hard Money Raised Out of White House:

Al Gore may have made false statements to investigators, which is illegal. Gore insisted he did not discuss hard money with investigators but Strauss's notes taken at the meeting show the figures 65% soft and 35% hard, which is how, according to campaign guidelines, money is added up for advertising. Janet Reno used Al Gore's cooperation with investigators and his apparent naivete when she cited how hard and soft money is not sufficient reason to prosecute through an appointment of an independent counsel. Another successful delay by this administration. Gore had earlier insisted that his soliciting of money for the Clinton-Gore reelection out of the White House through forty-five calls were for soft money only. Some money was reported back in 1997 by the Washington Post as being placed in hard money accounts back then Watergate's Woodward said to follow the money trail.

The House Government Reform Oversight Committee voted on August 6, 1998, to hold Janet Reno in contempt of Congress for refusing to turn over information she had in the form of memos from investigators. Looking into this matter for over two years. Because of the nature of the law, Janet Reno is more likely to appoint an independent counsel to look at Ickes who headed the Clinton-Gore effort if what might have occurred at these meetings with the President comes out.

With the Al Gore and H. Ickes roles in campaign alleged illegality progressing, Janet Reno is looking at evidence that Bill Clinton had control of the DNC campaign ads, which are funded by soft money and do not suppose to represent an individual candidate. Hatch and Lott have both expressed their discontent with Janet Reno's failure to appoint an independent counsel. But the cases are moving to court with indictments and the investigations are bring new insight into this misconduct. Thompson also called for an overall independent counsel to look at these charges instead of very specific defined inquirers. They want a review of the big picture and how the administration set out to violate the statutes early on.

In October 1998, in the Charlie Trie case, an important pretrial District Court ruling came down. A judge ruled that soft money is not covered by the exclusion of foreign money in U.S. elections. This is a major decision that may be appealed because most of the funds were soft money.

Al Gore was questioned on November 11, 1998, about his role in campaign funds raising and if he illegally benefited from the process. The forty-five or forty-six calls originating from government property are possible fraud.

Janet Reno had until December 7, 1998, to decide whether to ask three federal judges to appoint an independent counsel regarding issue advocacy ads and other fund raising activities. The Vice President released a statement that he would cooperate fully with Justice Department investigators. The Federal Elections Commission has recommended that the President's reelection campaign return $13.4 million for violating rules in the "issue ads" or "advocacy ads." Clinton is also defending his fund raising phone calls from the White House. David Kendall, his attorney in this matter, kept assuring the Justice Department that Bill, an attorney and running his second presidential campaign, did not know laws were being broken.

On December 7, 1998, Janet Reno announced that no independent counsel would be appointed to investigate President Clinton or Al Gore in the use of $46 million in ads paid for by the Democratic Party. She said they had relied on attorneys with every "issue ad" and claimed that the ads promoted the candidates. But J. Reno said you need to prove a deliberate attempt was made to violate the law. Both Al Gore and Bill Clinton were questioned. The White House response was that they had complied with the spirit and letter of the law. Both Fred Thompson and Dan Burton objected to Reno's finding and pointed to a clear conflict of interest.

Embassy Spokesman Denies Allegations:

The New York Times reports on Tuesday, December 15, 1998, that lawyers and investigators are saying federal authorities have new evidence that China was trying to "enhance the political standing" of those passing the money to Democratic campaigns to give them leverage in arguing for trade and technology projects.

Loral:

Representative Cox is investigating the role of campaign contributions by Loral, and may have a link to them helping the Chinese military rocket program. Bernard Schwartz of Loral was the biggest single contributor to the Clinton reelection campaign with $1 million, and Hughes donated to both Republican and Democratic campaigns. China had rockets to launch satellites or ICBMs that were less than reliable. And U.S. commercial companies helped their rocket program so China could launch their communications satellites. Included was guidance software that can be used to target ICBMs on U.S. cities more accurately than before. It is possible to separate out software to put satellites in proper orbit from software to target long-range missiles that are capable of delivering nuclear warheads. Two completely different types of orbits/trajectory could have been separated out but this was not done. And a waiver ordered by the White House run through the Commerce Department accomplished this when the usual channels denied the technology transfer. The Pentagon objected to the sale, and the U.S. State Department refused to grant the technology transfer. But the White House granted the waiver through the Commerce Department. Congress, in the summer of 1998, placed an embargo on additional technology being transferred to China, due in part to the rocket and guidance system, but also in response to China selling missile technology to Pakistan and Iran. This created an imbalance between India and Pakistan and we had aboveground nuclear tests in both countries for a period of time. An example of how important such technology can be.

Christopher Cox's special report was released on December 30, 1998, a 700-page classified report with a 9-0 vote of support. The five Republicans and four Democrats sent a nonpartisan report for leaders of Congress and the White House on the transfer of technology to China. It focused on China's attempts to gain U.S. military technology through intelligence. They said they looked at more serious matters than the Loral and Hughes help to transfer missile technology including high end computers but proposed that the Pentagon and State Department play more of a role in export licensing instead of using the Commerce Department like the Clinton administration did to get around restrictions.

The Justice Department was probing into Loral's documents to see if there was a link to 1996 campaign contributions over $600,000. Lim, an employee of Loral of Chinese descent, was granted a security waiver, enabling him to access long-range missile technology. The House voted overwhelmingly to block anymore transfer of technology to China before the presidential summit in 1998. J. Huang is now implicated in laundering money for the Clinton reelection campaign. J. Huang may have used his influence with the U.S. Commerce Department to interfere with investigations. A position he received from the White House after being with the DNC. Huang held a top-secret clearance at the Commerce Department, another case of insufficient background checks. One can't help but wonder if the White House did not waive it as they had for new staff at the White House, according to Gary Aldrich, FBI agent in charge of backgrounds at the White House. Huang, who received his security clearance while still at Lippo and carried it with him to DNC, received thirty-seven intelligence briefings on China while at the Commerce Department.

Damage:

United States Intelligence reports the Chinese military is developing a laser-type antisatellite weapons "ASATS." The United States and Russia have the technology but agree not to deploy it. It can compromise U.S. surveillance satellites that monitor military deployments and missile launches. Now this matter is a subject for future negotiations with agreements that will need to be reached by future administrations.

Lott said, "It is time to end the stonewalling and get to the truth." In reference to the new evidence of the Chinese government influencing the 1996 elections, Shelby, chairman of the Senate Select Committee on Intelligence, confirmed there is new information.

China, being a communist country where the government owns and operates the banks and business, was known and has been shown to Congress. To have had an interest in trying to influence the United States elections for the purpose of getting technology to their military and business. It is clear these players, long-time friends of Bill's, were operating on behalf of the Chinese government with large donations to both the DNC and the 1996 presidential campaign. But did Bill know where his long-time Chinese friends were getting the large capital to help finance his reelection? Will never be found in writing. He did accept it and returned the money when it was reported as coming from overseas. It is clear, unlike the soft hard money and "issue ads," that it is illegal to accept foreign money in a United States election. The President said he did not know. But did he ask or did he need to? Should we expect that before accepting millions? Maybe we should require better verification and reporting of large donations made to our future campaigns. In late May 1999 John Huang and Charlie Trie both entered plea deals with no indication that they surrendered any evidence that would bring charges against this administration or the DNC. Huang's agreement only involves small contributions to the Democrats in 1993 and 1994, out in California. Janet Reno's Justice has portrayed the Democratic Party and Clinton-Gore reelection campaigns as victims in their dealing and acceptance of funds that were returned when determined illegal. Now this administration will not have the embarrassment of a trial and everyone is off the hook in this matter with over $30 million in tax dollars spent. This was when the bipartisan Cox report came out that detailed lax security and the vastness of the amount of nuclear weapons secrets stolen on their watch. It was a good time to have these investigations quiet for good as we learn how repeated requests for simple wire-taps that could have exposed this matter sooner and stopped some of it were turned down by her office. All the while, the President had told us on more than one occasion in the last year that he was unaware of any secrets being stolen.

V. Kathleen Willey

Kathleen Willey is a wife and mother and who been a long-time supporter and activist in the Democratic Party. She signed on to the Clinton campaign as a campaign worker. She alleges that she was groped by the President in an unwanted advance. She was asking him for a more significant and higher-paying position. She had financial trouble and her husband committed suicide that day about the time of the encounter.

There was a prior flirting incident although this is the White House. Often it is acceptable etiquette to make minor overtures in an office. It is often interpreted as a personal acceptance and compliance with your boss. But this probably was a case where, on federal property and in a official capacity in the Oval Office. The President pushed himself on an employee in a manner well beyond reasonable behavior. It would be considered sexual harassment under the law. She was there with a serious need and venerable with a financial need. Her rights were violated and this matter could have very well continued unaddressed. If it was not the only incident and the Paula Jones subpoenas did not come down. They had become experts in keeping such encounters quiet.

The promiscuity would have been personal and between him and his family. If had not occurred on tax-payer property and on their time. The use of authority granted by elected office as governor and now as our Commander in Chief is considerable. This, coupled with the power an attorney projected at workers, must be very intimidating to a woman subject to that kind of environment.

Kathleen and Paula both kept quiet after their initial experiences. Powerful people can bring real trouble. The Paula Jones depositions and Monica Lewinsky brought Kathleen's story to the surface. But I got hospitalized for contacting the press.

Kathleen in her deposition of January 10, 1998.

Jones lawyers had carefully prepared a detailed list of questions. Thay walked through the entire incident. Some of it is as follows:

By Mr. Campbell:

Q. Ms. Willey, you've just been handed Deposition Exhibit 1, which is the Michael Isakoff Newsweek article that I was referring to. If you'll look down at the bottom of the left-hand corner of the first page of Exhibit 1 you'll see it says Newsweek, August 11, 1997. Do you see that?

A. Yes.

Q. It's correct, is it not, that you have read the Newsweek article before?

A. Yes.

Q. You do know the subject matter of the article; is that right?

A. Yes.

Q. And you know that the subject matter of the article, which is Exhibit 1, discusses an alleged incident between you and Mr. Clinton in the White House; is that right?

A. Yes.

Q. So that when I during this deposition refer to the incident, will you understand with me that I am referring to the alleged incident that is mentioned in this Newsweek article that is Deposition.

A. Yes.

Q. Now, Ms. Willey, did you talk to anyone about giving your testimony today in this deposition?

MR. GECKER: I assume you mean other than counsel?

MR. CAMPBELL: Anyone.

A. To him.

Q. You talked to your counsel, Mr. Gecker?

A. Yes.

Q. Did you talk to anyone else about your testimony today?

A. No.

Q. And that would include no one from Mr. Bennett's office; is that right?

A. Correct.

Q. And no one from Mr. Bill Bristov's office, who is the other attorney representing the other defendant in this case; is that right?

A. Correct.

Q. And is it correct that you did not talk to Mr. Clinton about giving your testimony here today?

A. That's correct.

Q. Would you please, ma'am, describe for us -- and I'm going to take you through in narrative fashion exactly what happened, if anything, is what I'm referring to as the incident. Do you understand me when I say that now?

A. Yes.

Q. Were you involved in any way in the incident?

A. Yes.

Q. On the occasion that is reported in Exhibit 1, did you go to see Mr. Clinton?

A. Yes.

Q. And to the best of your recollection, what date was that?

A. November 29, 1993.

Q. And what was the purpose of your visit to Mr. Clinton?

A. To discuss my need for a paid position.

Q. At the White House?

A. Yes.

Q. With the federal government?

A. Yes.

Q. And where did you see Mr. Clinton?

A. In the Oval Office.

Q. Within the White House?

A. Yes.

In President Clinton's January 17, 1998, deposition:

Q. Do you know why she would tell a story like that if it weren't true?

A. No, sir, I don't know. (He goes on about her financial problems how she was upset on the way in. He admits to putting his arms around her and maybe even kissing her. But that is all.)

Comment: There is some recall of the event.

The count moves forward:

Kissing, Hug, touching her breast and placing her hand on his genitals. Line by line.

Q. And then what happened?

A. Then he hugged me again and said that they would try to help me.

Q. And was that at the door in the private hallway leading back into the Oval Office?

A. Yes.

Q. And please describe the exact physical nature of the hug.

A. It was a hug.

Q. Is that all? Just an embrace?

A. It was a hug.

It continues with the kiss and placing of her hand on his genitals. Willey was not forthcoming but apparently not lying either. The statement "Just a big hug," "I don't think so," and "I can't remember." The vagueness of these responses is an attempt to play this down as we see in her numerous gifts and notes over the years. She flattered him in a personal manner. We don't know what were in her eyes as she walked into his office. How much she may have led him on. He has a reputation of rewarding sexual favors. His forward moves are believable, but I would like to know if she wears expensive perfume and smiles all the time.

Bill's Response, January 17:

Q. Did you ever attempt to kiss her on the lips?

A. No.

Q. Did you ever attempt to touch her breasts?

A. No.

Q. And you're aware that she testified that you took her hand and put it on your penis?

A. I'm aware of that.

White House reasoning: These were not attempts. He actually did.

Q. All right, and you deny that testimony?

A. I emphatically deny it. It did not happen.

After hearing this, you think about calling Solomon in. She is a mature fifty-year-old woman but attractive. They can take care of themselves. Could she not have just stepped back. Or was there any mention of a push off by her. I hear "I just resisted." More than once and she never claims to even say just no. At any point and the hug at the start. Did she hug back?

I think so. I mean, I think so; I mean, I don't really recall if I did or not. Please. But if he moved her hand it might have been too much too fast and she did then as she said. At that point she decided to leave the office.

Bill's response, January 17, 1998:

Q. Did you at any time have any form of sexual relations with Kathleen Willey?

A. No, I didn't.

White House reasoning: This is not a relationship although, now after all this! He now admits to remembering her but denies the incident completely. This is clear in the case of Paula Jones to this day. It is also well known I have a son. Relatives, friends, many doctors, others in South Florida and even on the Hill in Washington for years now. But they are still claiming no Shawn. The Paula Jones and my case that proceeded, any criminal problems, they have now. Are simple civil cases easily cleared up for years. If he would just apologize in response to her claim. It would have taken all the wind out of the case and removed most of the political damage. Kathleen Willey would never have surfaced. All she wanted was a public apology. I worked in private to see my son and offered in writing much more than Florida laws would have given Anna in child support. But now they face possible contempt and perjury charges. A handwritten note to Bill from her position in the Social Office. A little personal at the end but then she works in the Social Office.

His Reply:

June 5th 1993

WHITE HOUSE

5/93
SUBSTITUTION
Dear Kathleen

I love the tie. Thanks. I already have my shoes from Johnson and Murphy. Since they're located in Nashville, Tenn, and know I'm an Elvis fan, they also sent me a pair of blue suede shoes.

Best.

Bill

It is important to note that Katheen Willey, just a few weeks before the incident, gave Mr. Clinton a copy of a book that she read and he was mentioned in.

The hand written note to Bill.

Kathleen Willey

Dear Mr. President --

I just finished this book and thought that you'd enjoy it, if for no other reason than the fact that you just happen to be one of the characters!

I enjoyed being able to talk with you the day you left from the South Lawn. I hope you are well ---

Kathleen

October 12, 1993

Then he wrote back the following letter:

THE WHITE HOUSE
WASHINGTON
October 13, 1993

Kathleen Willey
2320 Castlebridge Road
Midlothian, Virginia 23113

Dear Kathleen:

Thanks for your note and for giving me a copy of Jeffrey Archer's Honor Among Thieves. I appreciate your sharing it with me, and I look forward to reading it.

Sincerely,

BILL

"Honor Among Thieves," you have to realize when you deal with these people that they like to flaunt thier cheating and misdeeds. They like taking risks. The excitement from pulling something off drives their actions. Kathleen had been involved in campaigning for the Democratic Party. I had been friends with employees of Democrats. They justify themselves by saying the Republicans have more money so we have to outsmart them.

Note from Kathleen Willey asking for the November 29, 1993, meeting:

Dear Mr. President:

What a wonderful week you have had! Congratulations on all of your well deserved success.

I would very much like to have a few minutes of your time to discuss something of importance to me.

I will want to hear from you ---

Fondly.

Kathleen

There was something going there. Did Kathleen know of Bill's history for engaging women for sex and did she attempt to apply it to get work? She has been working on it. Did she tell her husband, I will sleep with him if I have to in order to get a good position. They needed money. That is why she made the appointment.

An interesting note on December 5, 1995, requesting a new meeting for work. "That working on the campaign would be mutually beneficial to us both." And "few minutes of time" the fondly at the close before her signature is back. The same day a three-page note closing with fondly again.

Kathleen Willey

Dear Nancy --

I will be coming to Washington next Monday December 11th for two days and would like to talk to the President for a few minutes if that would be at all possible.

I would like to talk to him about the possibility of working on his reelection campaign. I would be able to move to Washington as soon as possible and feel that working on the campaign would be mutually beneficial to us both.

I know that this is a busy time for you and am most appreciative for any effort you would make on my behalf.

I hope to see you next week.

Fondly,

Kathleen

On December 21, 1995, the President writes back about her request for a new meeting. Note: Bill Clinton is not using White House on top of the letter. This is not the letterhead of the President. Is it personal or official? Mike McCurry said they could not find them because they could not decide just that.

Quaint, some of these letters are addressed to her home.

Bill Clinton
December 21, 1995

Kathleen Elizabeth Willey
2320 Castlebridge Road
Midlothian, Virginia 23113

Dear Kathleen:

Thanks for your letter of December 5, I'm sorry I missed you when you were in town last week, but it was good to hear from you and to get an update on your activities. The Convention on Biological Diversity must have been fascinating.

Thanks, too, for your continued desire to serve the administration. I'm glad to hear you're already not with Brian Baley and Ann Lewis regarding a job with the campaign. It sounds like you're on the right track.

Have a wonderful holiday season.

Sincerely,

Bill Clinton

These two could be back at it. Too bad the Paula Jones subpoenas came along and broke so much up.

Leaving Oval Office:

There is some discrepancy in some who saw Katheen leave the Oval Office and those she might have talked to about the incident.

One must keep in mind she is a real loyalist. The Jones deposition put her and others in an intensely difficult position. Their whole political future and financial situation were at risk. You can feel that you are betraying the United States government and they might have felt it is as important to keep quiet as about this as any national secret. Tripp, in her tapes with Monica Lewinsky, tells how she believes Kathleen because it is hard to fake whisker burns on the side of your face.

There is a pattern common to all these offenses deceit, denial and defiance, until you have them to the wall, like DNA or tape recordings. Is there obstruction of justice here? An attempt to keep her quiet. Coverup. A reversal of stories we know. Tripp asked by Monica on the tapes to come on board and lie.

In November 1998, Starr's prosecutors had been calling in witnesses to the grand jury in Alexandria to study Willey's claims. She was intimidated and influenced as a result of her testimony last year. Clinton, in his August 17 grand jury testimony, claimed, that he did not grope her. "I didn't do any of that," he said. "She was not telling the truth." Julie H. Steele, a close friend, said Willey ask her to lie, but there is something, about her taking the Fifth. And the story she told Steele is the same account of what happened that day. Clinton's lawyers also failed to turn over correspondence from Willey in response to the Paula Jones subpoena in January.

Willey had a relationship with a Democratic fundraiser named Nathan Landow with definite ties to the White House. Willey denied anyone tried to influence her testimony in her Paula Jones deposition but later amended it to say Landow "discussed my upcoming deposition with me." Landow took the Fifth in this matter and refused to testify this summer when called to court on the Willey matter. He is asking for immunity. Starr, in November

1998, continues to investigate Landow a developer, for his possibly influencing Kathleen and reported fund raising practices.

On January 7, 1999, Julie Steele is charged with three counts of obstruction of justice and one count of making false statements. She had backed Kathleen Willeys story, then contested it, saying in a Jones affidavit that Willey asked her to lie about when she told her about the Oval Office visit. Was she approached by some friends of the White House? Did she develop a need to discredit Kathleen to help the White House? Why would Kathleen tell Steele the story and then ask her to lie about when she first told her? The jury became deadlocked and the judge ordered a mistrial. Starr has decided not to recharge her. Kathleen has remained constant with her account over the years, even under questioning.

VI. Paula Jones Deposition and the Lie

Paula Jones's sexual harassment lawsuit brought subpoenas down on the White House employees. Monica and Bill's secret affair was about to become part of a legal coverup. Tripp, who had been though the Foster incident, had seen Willey after she came out of the Oval Office with her incident, and remembered a more pleasant times for her when the Bushes were in the White House, was now over in the Pentagon with Monica. They had become friends and Monica could not stop telling her about her relationship with the President. Tripp, in order to protect herself and with the possibility of later book deal began to tape the phone calls between Monica and her for over twelve hours. Since Monica would not talk to the press they were the best sources into the illicit affair at first.

The contents of the tapes were not fully released until well into the scandal. But I will present them here. So we can have what the players in this drama knew, when they were making their decisions.

Tripp Tapes:

Tripp: I know. It seems unfair. It seems grossly unfair, actually. Well, he's into kind of a denial anyway. I mean he denied Kathleen Willey to you.

Lewinsky: Yeah.

Tripp: And do I believe he harassed her? Of course not. I mean in the true sense of the world, the word, of course, not. Do I think he kissed her? Yeah.

Lewinsky: You know.

Tripp: It's hard to fake beard burn. Thank God, I didn't say that.

Lewinsky: Hah.

Lewinsky: I'm just -- I'm starting to get a little nervous about Vernon.

Tripp: Why?

Lewinsky: I don't know. I--uh - I think - I just want everything to be easy. I want him to call me and say. "You know, how does this amount of money, doing this here sound?" And I say. "that's sound great." He says, "Okay. Consider it a done deal."

Tripp: Mm-hmm.

Here Monica Lewinsky is upset because the President is not interested in her anymore and she is not content with her Pentagon position.

Tripp: It's like -- it makes you sound demented or something. I mean, it makes you -- uh -- I that just angers me beyond belief. But it certainly keeps him in the clear. "Hey, we had to get her out of here, she was stalking me."

Tripp: This navy blue dress. Now all I would say to you is. I know how you fell today and I know why you fell the way you do today, but you have a very long life ahead of you. I would rather you had that in your possession if you need it years from now. That's all I'm gonna say.

She goes on to tell how long the proof will last. And how down the road you may need it if he calls her a stalker.

Lewinsky: I'm not going to get in trouble. I will not get in trouble. Because you know what? The story I signed under oath. Is what someone else is saying under oath.

Tripp: Who?

Lewinsky: He will.

Tripp: Oh, the big guy. Of course.

Lewinsky: The people said nothing happened but he.

Tripp: And you are positive. A hundred percent positive.

That he is not going to slip up when he gets his deposition.

Lewinsky: Him.

Tripp: Well, he is only human. He is only human.

It is clear Monica is working with the White House to get the story down. They are both going to lie if this matter comes up. It worked until the existence of tapes came out in late January.

Tripp: Because that's huge. Vernon Jordan.

Lewinsky: What is he, what is it he will, do for me.

Tripp: Look, he knows you are putting all your. Legally it is fighting. But you are putting everything on the line. Lying under oath. He knows you did that.

Lewinsky: I already did. I signed it.

This is why she needed immunity from Starr. She had landed a good-paying job for her silence and cooperation. In December 1997, Jones's attorneys subpoena M. Lewinsky. Monica Lewinsky's affidavit. She received a subpoena on December 19, 1997. With the affidavit taken January 7, 1998, and handed over to Paula Jones' attorneys on January 16, 1998. It was not released until March 13, 1998, to fight a motion to dismiss their case by Clinton's attorneys.

Excerpt:

I have never had a sexual relationship with the President, he did not propose that we have a sexual relationship, he did not offer me employment or other benefits in exchange for a sexual relationship, he did not deny me employment or other benefits for rejecting a sexual relationship. I do not know of any other person who had a sexual relationship with the President, was offered employment or other benefits in exchange for a sexual relationship, or was denied employment or other benefits for rejecting a sexual relationship. The occasions that I saw the President after I left employment at the White House in April, 1996, were official receptions, formal functions or events related to the U.S. Department of Defense, where I was working at the time. There were other people present on those occasions.

I declare under the penalty of perjury that the foregoing is true and correct.

(signed)

Monica S. Lewinsky

You can see why her attorneys wanted full immunity before she talked to Ken Starr and his people. This document was prepared by attorneys for Bill Clinton and presented to Monica by them. It is what was referred to in Tripp's tapes as a lie that the President was going to backup a clear attempt to obstruct justice.

January 12, Tripp informs Starr of her taping.

January 13, Tripp wears FBI wire and meets with Monica.

January 14, Tripp turns over talking points to Starr.

January 16, She meets with one of Paula Jones's legal team and tells them about Bill and Monica's relationship.

Tripp and Monica Talking Points:

There are at least three versions of the talking points. The third is presented below.

1. By the way, remember how I said there was someone else that I knew about. Well, she turned out to be a huge liar. I found out she left the White House because she was stalking the President or something like that. Well, at least that gets me out of another scandal I know about.

It is hard to believe that Tripp did not have some input in this statement with the last line especially "get me out of another scandal." What other party would want that statement in there?

2. The first few paragraphs should be about me -- what I do now, what I did at the White House and for how many years I was there as a career person and as a political appointee.

3. Kathleen and I were friends. At around the time of her husband's death, she came to me after she allegedly came out of the Oval Office and looked _____, I don't recall her exact words, but she claimed at the time _____ and was very happy. This is the issue about which Tripp was in dispute with the Presidents attorney and her reason why she taped because he called her a liar on this matter. They all had to get their stories the same for the depositions coming up.

4. I did not see her go in or see her come out.

5. Talk about when I became out of touch with her and maybe why.

6. The next time I heard of her was when a Newsweek reporter showed up in my office saying she was naming me as someone who would corroborate that she was sexually harassed by the President. I spoke with her that evening, etc. and she relayed to me a sequence of events that was very dissimilar from what I remembered happening. As a result of my conversation with her and subsequent reports that showed she had tried to enlist the help of someone else in her lie that the President sexually harassed her, I now do not believe that what she claimed happened really happened. I now find it completely plausible that she herself smeared her lipstick, untucked her blouse, etc. It is clear that the author(s) here are trying to discredit K. Willey's story but it seems to acknowledge there was a meeting and as she exited the Oval Office her lipstick was smeared and blouse disturbed.

7. I never saw her go into the Oval Office or come out of the Oval Office.

8. I have never observed the President behave inappropriately with anybody.

We know Monica and Linda were discussing the upcoming Paula Jones deposition concerning sexual harassment. And the White House had taken its positions. With Monica going it alone, she was getting good job offers, that is what she wanted out of it. Tripp, at this time, had tapes so she could defend her position if the White House pressured her about the Monica affair with the President. It is interesting in a town where everyone is trying to get something on everyone else, and it is a good employee who doesn't see or hear everything. The phone conversations went on for a long time. And apparently there are e-mail reports and discussions in the Pentagon's computer system. Everyone knew that employers often checked their personal e-mail and even listened in on phone conversations. That Monica went on so much could have been the result of youth and innocence but Tripp must have known there was a risk this might come back on them.

Deposition and Lie:

They discussed the need for specific questions because of the definition of sex. And the right to question as the law that Bill had signed and supported that allows accusers of sexual harassment to ask questions about other sexual encounters to see if there is a pattern of behavior.

Definition of sexual relations as defined by Jones's attorneys:

For the purposes of this deposition, a person engages in "sexual relations" when the person knowingly engages in or causes:

(1) contact with the genitalia, anus groin, breast, inner thigh, or buttocks of any person with an intent to arouse or gratify the sexual desire of any person.

(2) contact between any part of the person's body or an object and the genitals or anus of another person, or

(3) contact between the genitals or anus of the person and any part of another person's body "Contact" either directly or through clothing.

The questioning starts with Kathleen Willey and her alleged encounter but the President responds to each question of specifically touching any part of her body with no, and no to any sexual relationship. Questioning is also about possible very good job offers well beyond her means.

Then the questioning moves to Monica and he barely remembers her as an intern who was transferred to the Pentagon.

Q. Is it true that when she worked at the White House she met with you several times?

A. I don't know about several times. There was a period when the, when the Republican Congress shut the government down that the whole White House was being run by interns, and she was assigned to work back in the Chief of Staff's office, and we were all working there, and so I saw her on two or three occasions, then, and then when she worked at the White House, I think there were one or two other times when she brought some documents to me.

What must have started going through Bill's head at this point.

Q. Well, you also saw her at a number of social functions at the White House, didn't you?

A. Could you be specific? I'm not sure. I mean when we had, when we had like big staff things for, if I had a, like in the summertime, if I had a birthday party and the whole White House staff came, then she must have been there. If we had a Christmas party and the whole White House staff was invited, she must have been there. I don't remember any specific social occasions at the White House, but people who work there when they're invited to these things normally come. It's a -- they work long hours, it's hard work, and it's one of the nice things about being able to work there, so I assume she was there, but I don't have any specific recollection of any social events. A real nice talk around. Then Judge Wright asks for a lunch break. It must have been apparent that Bill was on the spot and perhaps this was a chance to consider the surprise before questioning proceeded.

Q. Mr. President, before the break, we were talking about Monica Lewinsky. At any time were you and Monica Lewinsky together alone in the Oval Office?

A. I don't recall, but as I said, when she worked at the legislative affairs office, they always had somebody there on the weekends, Sometimes they'd bring me things on the weekends. She-- it seems to me she brought things to me once or twice on the weekends. In that case, whatever time she would be in there, drop it off, exchange a few words and go, she was there. I don't have any specific recollections of what the issues were, what was going on, but when the Congress is there, we're working all the time, and typically I would do some work on one of the days of the weekends in the afternoon.

Q. So I understand, your testimony is that it was possible, then that you were alone with her, but you have no specific recollection of that ever happening?

A. Yes. That's correct. It's possible that she in, in, while she was working there, brought something to me and that at the time she brought it to me, she was the only person there. That's possible.

They knew for months that Monica had been subpoenaed and had signed an affidavit saying she did not have any sexual relationship with Bill Clinton. Gifts from her were returned and witnesses to her visits, like Betty Currie, talked to. He at this point had already lied under oath. But later they claim that the Oval office is part of the White House like denial of being alone in the hotel room with Paula Jones was not a lie because the Oval Office, like the hotel room, is part of a bigger structure and people might be there.

Q. Did she tell you she had been served with a subpoena in this case?

A. No. I don't know if she had been.

Q. Did you ever talk with Monica Lewinsky about the possibility that she might be asked to testify in this case?

A. Bruce Lindsey, I think Bruce Lindsey told me that she was. I want to be as accurate as I can.

He goes on to say how Betty Currie might have talked with her and about finding work for her too. They had covered the personal visits to the White House. And the President was sticking to his story that he never talked to her about this case. Very important, too because his attorneys had her sign an affidavit saying she never had a sexual relationship with the President specifically because this deposition was coming up.

Q. Recently you took a trip that included a visit to Bosnia, correct.

A. That's correct.

Q. While you were on that trip, did you talk to Monica Lewinsky?

A. I don't believe she was on that trip.

Q. Did you talk to her on the telephone?

A. No.

We know she did call him from Washington. She had a number that got through. The conversation was concerning ending their relationship.

Q. You know a man named Vernon Jordan?

A. I know him well.

Q. You've know him for a long time?

A. A long time.

Q. Has it ever been reported to you that he met with Monica Lewinsky and talked about this case?

A. I knew that he met with her. I think Betty suggested that he meet with her. Anyway, he met with her. I, I thought they he talked to her about something else. I didn't know that -- I thought he had given her some advice about her move to New York. Seem like that's what Betty said.

I wonder if they ever talk on the golf course. I heard in their first term from Unlimited Access that people in thier party would use the Marine helicopter as a golf cart going from shot to shot.

I bet there were good conversations about this time.

Q. Is it your understanding that she was offered a job in the U.N.?

A. I know that she interviewed for one. I don't know if she was offered one or not.

This is the second part of the pattern Paula Jones's attorneys are trying to establish. Reward in the form of work for sex. We know now that Monica Lewinsky really lobbied hard for good-paying work. And that she had confidence in Bill that, from the Linda Tripp tapes, he would lie for sure as she did on the affidavit that Vernon Jordan knew she signed.

They went over the gifts they had exchanged. Some they tried to get back and asked Betty Currie to retrieve them. Betty doesn't get paid enough.

Q. Did you have an extramarital sexual affair with Monica Lewinsky?

A. No.

Q. If she told someone that she had a sexual affair with you beginning in November of 1995, would that be a lie?

A. It's certainly not the truth. It would not be the truth.

Q. I think I used the term "sexual affair." And so the record is completely clear, have you ever had a sexual relations with Monica Lewinsky, as that term is defined in Deposition Exhibit 1 as modified by the Court?

A. I have never had a sexual relations with Monica Lewinsky. I've never had an affair with her.

There it is, the lie that was sold to us for over seven months.

Next we get into the denial of being alone with Paula Jones and a series of other women when he was alone at thier residence or the Governor's residence. Some received work directly from Bill.

Gennifer Flowers is the best known of these women and wrote Bill a letter asking for work. She also claims a twelve-year relationship.

Q. Eventually Gennifer Flowers was hired to work as a state employee for the Arkansas Board of Review Appeals Tribunal, correct?

A. That was __ some months after this, that's right. I believe that's right. I think several months after that she did get a state job. Which was a few months after then and a few years after the first letter.

He admits to one sexual encounter with Gennifer Flowers.

Q. On how many occasions?

A. Once.

Q. In what year?

A. 1977.

On January 21, 1998, the Washington Post breaks the story of Monica Lewinsky, an intern having an affair with the President.

January 26, 1998:   West Wing, Roosevelt Room, President Clinton said,   "I did not have sexual relations with that woman, Ms. Lewinsky. I never told anybody to lie. Not a single time. Never. These allegations are false. And I need to go back to work for the American people." He came across emotionally like he was hurt that people would think this affair took place and really told us these allegations were false. Looked right into camera and shook his finger at the American people. In an intense fashion.

January   28,   1998,   Hillary's   morning   talk   show appearance: She says she believes her husband and tells how Vernon Jordan has gotten jobs for so many people and how they have friends. Then her famous claim: "The great story here for some to find it and write about it and explain it is this is a vast right wing conspiracy that has been conspiring against my husband since the day he announced for President."

February 6, 1998, Betty Currie: This model secretary since 1992, with reports in the New York Times and the Washington Post that he called her in to go over what to say in possible testimony. He denied trying to influence her memory. "I never told anybody to do anything but tell the truth" were made to the press when he was with Tony Blair, the British Prime Minister.

March 1998, Senator Lott: On CNBC's "HardBall", talking to Lott he speaks of the President's problem as, "I do think he needs to get it behind him." And the best way is to tell the truth. Else the American people would have to deal with this. Chris Matthews first brought up the option of censuring the President for his conduct about this time.

June 16, also on "HardBall": Gennifer Flowers tells how even now after a court case, Bill and the White House made statements that there was no long affair and she had her attorney send them a letter that if they continue to make false statements that they would take action. They said that she doctored tapes that showed Bill getting her a job. Not just denial again but more defiance. She also made note that if you go against them. That you have to experience it yourself. How much pressure they can bring down on you. I can relate to that. They try and discredit you and can get quite high-handed. Turning the truth around is their real area of expertise.

With Monica about this time it is don't ask, don't tell strategy with the staff in the White House. "That woman" was the only way the President referenced her. She was more of a girl when he had his relationship with her. But they were careful not to offend her hoping she would stay on the team.

The Clintons announced they will still go to China, even against the urging of Democrats as well as Republicans in Congress. That they should wait until the foreign campaign contributions from a communist country. And the issue of transfer of military technology could be cleared up. Also in the face of more than 400 votes in Congress they continue to bring Chinese into the White House and refused to postpone their trip. Also, there was no explanation of foreign policy from the administration. Where was the voice of the human rights violations and actions on counterfeit software coming from China? Didn't the American public deserve to know what economic, political and strategic goals the United States has in its current and future relations with a country so important it has been given the red carpet right in to the White House many times in recent years? But it became a good trip for the White House. The President looked presidential and at the nation's business. They were back by July 4, then went to Miami again.

Then Tripp began to testify, putting pressure on Monica. Would she stick with the President? Then Starr would have to indict her. Better for Starr if she would flip and show the President had lied and if the tapes showed she had asked someone to lie. Not just sexual relationship, then there is obstruction too. We know that thirty-seven times she was cleared to the White House after she left. Monica made a statement about how she always has lied.

July 7, 1998: Court rules Secret Service employees must testify about what they know concerning Monica Lewinsky, the three judges ruling together. Treasury may appeal to Supreme Court. Clinton could give them the go-ahead to testify. If the White House was sincere as it claims it would move this matter along, like the President told us. We would get more instead of less, sooner instead of later.

While there had not been much effort at this point to discredit Monica Lewinsky, they didn't know if she was still loyal to them. It is clear that she was going to say there was some kind of sexual contact. But how far would she go to avoid prosecution? Maybe she was in love with the President. She was young enough to be vulnerable.

Tripp had seemed glad on the way in and out of her grand jury testimony with Ken Starr and her being betrayed as the villains by some. This is discovery material, broader than trial evidence. Bill is rallying, joe six pack and Hillary is complaining cable television for covering so much of this scandal that they can't rebut all of it. The White House with spin has changed the focus over to what type of person Linda Tripp is, questioning motives and character, but are holding back on Monica. With Tripp, Betty Currie and various Secret Service testifying, the pressure was on Monica and the White House. Because Clinton's attorneys file in Supreme Court to block further testimony from the Secret Service two branches of government are in conflict. Chief Justice William Rehnquist refuses to block agents from testifying and this clears the way for further testimony the following week. Evidence will be under seal until the full court hears the case. Senator Lott comments he could end this if he came forward. Mike McCurry, the Press Secretary through all this, is saying he knows nothing. Clinton is saying he wasn't alone with Monica Lewinsky. The Secret Service may know differently. With Paula Jones, the President says he wasn't alone with her in the hotel room. The reasoning is there were others in the hotel. Gennifer Flowers said the President told her, "You lie, I lie, and we are okay." Let's see what kind of reasoning will develop as this unfolds.

On July 28, 1998, Monica would get full immunity from Ken Starr before going to the grand jury for her full and truthful testimony including her mother's. She will not have to plead guilty. He may have given her full immunity because of her age and innocent type of affection or love for Bill. The next day, Clinton agrees to testify on videotape. Now Monica is going to testify to the truth. Linda Tripp talked the to press for the first time and told the American people "I am just like you."

The navy blue dress with semen stain is located. Apparently Monica's mother had it. The stain on it was DNA tested. It could be why she got immunity too. On August 3 the White House physician draws blood from the President for the comparison. If it is a DNA match, this will be hard evidence. How do they continue to lie their way out of this?

But the White House is saying the President is already telling the truth. No sexual relationship, no one asked to lie. The polls show that if he is just lying about sex, then he should not get impeached. But if it is also obstruction of justice then the public is for impeachment. The President is being urged by the press and politicians to come forward and get this behind him and come clean to the American people. Nevertheless, the White House states Bill is going to stand by his story. No sex, no one to lie. But this would be perjury in a grand jury. The Supreme Court ruling this week refuses to block White House attorneys from testifying. A former White House staffer says the President should come clean on Monica. But David Kendall, personal attorney, and Micky Kantor, political attorney, and Mrs. Clinton still hold to their positions.

New video of Monica Lewinsky at fund raising function is shown. Lewinsky was hanging out at the site early where the President was going to be. A man saw her and the Secret Service tells him that we are afraid she may try and kiss him. She reached out to grab him. He hugs her back. Hello, how are you, how is the new job doing. Fine.

About a week before the President is to testify, Monica gives her account of the events. Her long, detailed account of her sexual relationship with the President is believed. More people call for a complete apology. With DNA test results looming, seventy-five percent of the people believe Monica and Bill had an affair. A late warning to the President. You were not truthful in the January deposition but if you lie to the grand jury, it could be impeachable. Final reports out of the White House over the weekend. Bill is going to say there was some kind of sexual relationship.

August 17, 1998, grand jury testimony by President Clinton:

He takes the oath and answers yes to understanding oath in the Paula Jones case. Upon the first question concerning sex with Ms. Lewinsky, the President reads a prepared statement.

Clinton: When I was alone with Ms. Lewinsky on certain occasions in early 1996, and once in early 1997, I engaged in conduct that was wrong. These encounters did not consist of sexual intercourse. They did not constitute sexual relations, as I understood that term to be defined at my January 17th, 1998, deposition.

But they did involve inappropriate, intimate contact. These inappropriate encounters ended at my insistence in early 1997. I also had occasional telephone conversations with Ms. Lewinsky that included inappropriate sexual banter.

Q. Was this contact with Ms. Lewinsky -- Mr. President, did it involve any sexual contact in any way, shape or form?

Clinton: Mr. Bittman, I said in this statement I would like to stay to the term of the statement. I think it's clear what inappropriately intimate is. I have said what it did not include. It did not include sexual intercourse, and I did not believe this included conduct which falls within the definition I was given in the Jones deposition. And I would like to stay with that characterization.

The term "sexual contact" is defined as contact with certain body parts. And does not require sexual intercourse to have taken place. Thus his denial of touching Monica is how we get to who touched who. The President asks us to accept inappropriate intimate contact here as not including touching the specific body parts defined in the Jones definition. That he agreed to by the term "sexual relations" at the time of the trial.

They ask the President if he understands the term "sexual relations" in the Paula Jones case and that is to be used here to mean the same thing. He offers his understanding of the term.

Clinton: My understanding of this definition is that it covers contact by the person being deposed with the enumerated areas, if the contact is done with an intent to arouse or gratify. That's my understanding of the definition.

Question: What did you believe the definition to include and exclude? What kind of exclusions?

Clinton: I thought the definition included any activity by the person being deposed where the person who was the actor and came in contact with those parts of the body with the purpose or intent of gratification, and excluded any other activity. For example, kissing's not covered by that, I don't think.

What the President is asking us to believe is that she had "sexual relations" with him but he never touched her. And we should believe he was not lying or committing perjury when he said repeatedly that he had no sexual relationship of any shape or kind with Monica.

This was in response to his counsel, filing Ms. Lewinsky's false affidavit, saying that there was absolutely no sex of any kind in any manner, shape or form with the President.

The President explains that, "In the present tense, that's an accurate statement. That was an actual--that was an

91

accurate statement." Later he and his attorneys claim he was not focusing or paying attention at this time.

Question: The statement that there was no sex of any kind, in any manner, shape or form with President Clinton was an utterly false statement? Is that correct?

The President: It depends on what the meaning of the word "is" is. If "is" means is and never has been that's one thing. If it means there is none, that was a completely true statement.

An evasive response at best. He is later asked again if he touched specific body parts of Ms. Lewinsky.

Question: So touching, in your view then and now-- the person being deposed touching or kissing the breast of another person would fall within the definition?

Clinton: That's correct, sir.

Question: And you testified that you didn't have sexual relations with Monica Lewinsky in the Jones deposition, under that definition, correct?

Clinton: That's correct, sir.

Questions about the other body parts are answered the same no. The videotaped testimony ends. And David Kendall, the President's attorney, makes the statement.

"This afternoon, the President voluntarily testified for more than four hours about his relationship with Mrs. Lewinsky and the questions he was asked about that relationship in the Jones deposition last January. He testified truthfully. We are hopeful that the President's testimony will finally bring closure to the independent counsel's more than four year and over forty million dollar investigation which has culminated with an investigation of the President's private life."

Clinton's Apology after Grand Jury Testimony:

"I know that my public comments and my silence about this matter gave a false impression. I misled people, including even my wife. I deeply regret that."

The first part was what most characterized as an incomplete apology. The second half of it was an attack on the independent counsel Ken Starr, which many thought was inappropriate. He did not look good. He looked like he got caught. Some said, but sometimes defendants will not admit the truth in a case, even when the verdict has come down. For over seven months he had sent his people out but now with the DNA evidence, he could not talk around this. He had sent his attorneys and staff that he lied to out to lie for him and to the American people. He had lied to senators on this matter and sent out other surrogates, the troops to sell this lie, that there was no sex relationship with Monica Lewinsky.

On the following day, Monica Lewinsky was called to testify, apparently to clear up any discrepancies. Senator Hatch publicly said, if the President would just tell the truth, would be the best means to begin the end to this affair. Then Linda Tripp was also recalled to testify and there was talk of a possible impeachment after the election.

Some, like Sam Nunn, former Democrat from Georgia, and Jerry Falwell are calling for his resignation. Dick Gephardt was lied to face to face by the President. He and other Democrats on the Hill say it is time to stop and let's wait for the election. But it was going to be hard on him. Finally, just as the President headed for Russia, Trent Lott states, "As a husband and a father I am offended by the President's behavior and by the tragic example that he has set for the young people of this country. There is a moral dimension to the American presidency."

VII. Impeachment

On September 1, 1998, Mike McCurry leaves saying that he never had intentionally misled the press. If it seemed that way it was because his boss had done that to him. Some Democrats are expressing that they are "feeling betrayed." About a half-dozen Republicans call for resignation. This is before the Starr Report comes out. But apparently none has gone to the White House with that message. The President heads for Ireland. Some independent Democrats, like Joseph Lieberman of Connecticut and Pat Moynihan of New York, hit the President hard. This elicits a response from Clinton while overseas. He restates his regrets for misleading people.

October 9, 1998, morning meeting with Democrats: According to them, the President expressed remorse but there is no talk, as with Nixon, of resigning. But the report is not out and it is expected to contain impeachable material. Perhaps he comes across more sincere in private where he doesn't feel the pressure of the dignity of the office as in his public announcements.

The Starr Report hits the House under lock and key, 445 pages, with the DNA test reported positive from the stain on Monica's dress. The House Rules Committee soon votes to release the report. Bill is back and out at another campaign fund raiser.

This is the first time his wife introduced him since this affair surfaced in January. The President apologized to his cabinet for misleading them. A few more are asking for him to resign. There are eleven counts in the Starr Report but the perjury and obstruction of justice are the strongest areas.   According to David Kendall, the President's attorney, they are going to fight this. The President insists he did not lie. Even if legally valid, it may be a political problem.   He is receiving criticism from some foreign press. The First Lady is out again in New York. There is real trouble from Whitewater and Filegate and a call for a new independent counsel for campaign financing is in the background.

The First Family's supporters are trying to say that the report and matter is all about sex.   His lawyer and supporters are claiming no illegalities.   Posturing for a possible legal battle when he is out of office or a trial in the Senate if it goes that far. He had not addressed the American public that he lied under oath. In both his civil and grand jury testimony polls show nine out of ten think he lied in his depositions. If he were a CEO, university professor or judge, he would have been out by now.

Others are angered that he is still fighting this and if he comes forward at this time and admits in writing that he committed perjury, it should be accompanied with his resignation. Some say it is too late for just censure with this pattern of lying and misconduct that continues. Not until his back is absolutely up against the wall does he come forward. Look what he put his supporters through and how he used Betty Currie. Used a venerable Monica Lewinsky, no matter how willing she was. He offered to help get her work when he needed her to lie for him. Some go as far to say Monica was more of a service to him.

What have we all gone through with his unwillingness to come forward for seven months with the truth. How many surrogates lied to us and how many hours of debate, from supporters. All the time they were perpetuating a lie. He did not step forward to stop it. He could have remained silent or stuck with "it was a complicated relationship" or not commented. But he sent his forces out to win this battle like the previous ones. And Paula Jones's reputation and case were subverted. And what about Kathleen Willey? Also how may friends feel betrayed. What are other governments and newspapers joking about?

I have been a victim of lies from Hillary's mother and sister, been kept from my son and distraught over their disrespect for the court, the judge, and me. "There must be something wrong with the three branches of government that this has gone so far." This statement more than once came from Anna in court. And her mother backed her, lying. I felt, after the breaking of the perjury story in January, that now the country would see how they will lie and degrade even those who were loyal to them. They have a propensity for putting their needs and goals ahead of others' rights. Back in 1996, Thanksgiving, if she hadn't gone to the beach "they could have pulled this off." They let you know they're on top, in charge, and going to get their way.

Congress was preparing for impeachment hearings. Republicans were going to play this out. The President was campaigning around the country and raising a lot of money for candidates. Democrats in Congress would like expedited hearings like their constituents back in their districts. Women's organizations showed support for the President but made it a point to condemn his actions. Clinton was conducting the nation's business as he worked with leaders of the Middle East on a possible new agreement.

It is revealed that Dick Morris, after the affair with Monica Lewinsky, was exposed in the Jones deposition. And when Bill's testimony did not go well, he asked Morris

"What about the legal thing? You know, the legal thing." Morris's response: "This is not a legal process, it is a political thing." They took a poll which showed thirty-five percent of the people thought perjury by the President should result in jail. So "We have to win this thing."

On October 5, 1998, the House Judiciary Committee votes 21 for and 16 against, completely bipartisan. Now on to the full House. Hyde and the other Republicans could not get any Democrats to go along. Two days later, Bill and Hill are trying to reach Democrats to vote in their favor. Bill said, "I received a large number of calls from House members and I have tried to return their calls. I haven't been able to return them all because we have other things to do. Now I'll try and call the rest of them today. I think the votes will be a vote of principles. It is up to others to decide what happens to me. And hopefully it will be up to the American people to make a clear statement there."

Lying to the public was a count against Nixon who had resigned at this point. His actions were considered more serious by most and raised bipartisan objections. On October 8, 1998, the whole House voted for impeachment with only 31 against without a majority of support from the public polls. Congress persons are citing principles to support their positions.

The President responds, "Personally I am, I am fine. This is beyond my control. I have to work on what I can do. What I can do is my job, for the American people. I trust the American people, they almost always get it right for more than 220 years."

Bennett, the President's attorney, writes, to Judge Wright saying the affidavit he submitted in the Jones case was not completely true. Stating "Unavoidable ethical obligation to correct record." Betty Currie's deposition is released in October 1998, when the president got back from the Paula Jones deposition in January. He called Betty in on Sunday, and he said he had been asked questions about Monica Lewinsky. To what the President told her.

The best she said she could remember was:

"You were always there when Monica was there. We were never really alone."

Q. Did the President also make the statement "Monica came on to me, and I never touched her, right?"

Currie: Yes, that statement was made, sir.

Q. Did the President also state to you at that time that "She wanted to have sex with me, and I can't do that, right"?

Currie: I don't remember the "right" part coming after there. But probably without the "right."

Monday: Hatch mentioned he needed to settle the Paula Jones case and then address Kathleen Willey. You got the feeling Hatch was somewhat saddened or sorrowful at this point.

On CNBC's "HardBall", G. Gordon Liddy: How do you think this is going to sell? Some people want him to resign. He said he won't and I believe him. So, the only thing to do is continue the process and then a trial in the Senate. And that is how it should be.

Hyde is talking about processing maybe just three of the charges perjury, subordination of witness and abuse of power to move it along. But if there is not some type of confession of illegal activity, then they might need to go through witnesses.

What the White House needs now is some plea bargaining to get out of this dilemma. They are not able to come forward with the admission of breaking the law because they have to concern themselves with possible criminal charges.

A $1 million offer to Paula Jones is made to get her to settle so the country can move forward. If the President would admit this was wrong or apologize, it would be a political plus at this point. With these other allegations that also need to be resolved pending, it would get some of this behind him and make it easier to forgive him. There are a lot of people who would be encouraged by such a apology. And it would be a start in rebuilding of his integrity.

The military had to ask generals to stop personnel for making degrading statements about the President because the military should be apolitical. The President's brother, Roger, speaks out. It sounds like he made some improvements in his thinking. According to him, Bill helped him years ago before he went through his rethinking. He says it is when you start lying to yourself that it really gets dangerous. On October 23, 1998, a peace accord is reached in the Middle East. That weekend, Dick Morris on Fox says Bill came back after the Paula Jones deposition after going over his lying and perjury. He said, he did not do what they said I did. But I did do something. And I think I did so much. I think I can't prove I am innocent. Also, that it will come out after the next election the pressure put on these women by secret police. Dick Morris is the one, he asked to take a poll to see if they could sell his story to the American public.

In the last week of campaigning for the November elections this issue is a little old and does not directly apply to every candidate. Bill and Hill are going out separately not to draw attention to their relationship. There is attention to the issues and the President had a good week, with the Y summit agreement.

In the Paula Jones case, the judge releases about 900 pages. Current thinking is that the President is a realist and he will probably not win on appeal. And the judge's ruling could be overturned, which resulted in the case being dismissed on April 1, 1998. Finally, to have this closed before, House hearings would be a big plus. Hirschfeld of New York offers Paula Jones $1 million again to settle the case.

When the ballots were counted the Republicans lost five seats in the House. But they picked up as many governorships with a wash in the U.S. Senate. Every candidate Hillary campaigned for in the last weeks took off to victory. She still had the charm and could deliver. They wisely campaigned separately to avoid the moral stigma of Monica. Bill was able to bring in major capital to lots of congressional and gubernatorial races. The Republicans won the governors' races where candidates focused on the issues which was something lacking from this last Republican Congress. They gave in to Clinton in the final weeks of their session. It is clear that they did not go after Bill before the August 17, deposition. They should have spoken out on policy and pending legislation, a real missed opportunity for them. One got the feeling that they were afraid to comment on the scandal but wanted the scandal to carry them to victory.

With victory and Clinton's personal popularity high in regards to job performance, administration supporters talked about how Congress needed to define what an impeachable offense is before moving forward, while the White House was asking for an expedited hearing. What did they expect, a delay like on April 1, 1998, in the Paula Jones case? Because there is no punishment possible and therefore no crime, some kind of null prosecute ruling. And they could declare victory in regard to the Paula Jones case.

The facts were that they had impeachment proceedings that needed to be voted on by the full House. As mandated by the Constitution, they must proceed. It would be up to each member whether or not these actions rose to an impeachable offense and a vote placed by each. Hillary wrote a thirty-seven-page brief on what an impeachable offense is at the time of Watergate. Her brief concluded that perjury is impeachable with each member of the committee at that time signed on to it.

Hyde announces a scaled-down hearing to expedite, a consideration of public opinion and the wish of many of his own party in Congress to dispose of this matter as quickly as possible. He would call Ken Starr to present the evidence gathered and without witness. The committee sends eighty one questions to the White House so they can have a chance to clear this matter up. Some would require the admission of lying under oath. The White House says it will respond. Ironically Newt Gingrich is on his way out. The President's personal ratings are at an all-time low in moral standing, according to exit polls. But they like his work performance and those ratings are still high.

Bob Livingston is the man the House Republicans plan to elect for the new speaker. He is the Chairman of the House Appropriations Committee. He can compromise and was a prosecutor in the Navy. Newt Gingrich will even leave his House seat walking away from politics altogether. The man who helped build the new majority in the House could not deliver against this White House in this last session of Congress or election.

On November 9, 1998, the Supreme Court rules Bruce Lindsey and the Secret Service can testify. Bill will be questioned by the Justice Department with respect to campaign fund raising.

It may be necessary to hit Iraq, The King of Saudi Arabia will give support but no access to military facilities. Support from others in the area is weak. The image of America could be temporarily weakened to the extent other countries in the region are not giving this President the full cooperation he requests.

Dole again on CNBC, says how the Clinton campaign had serious money to throw at him early. And Janet Reno is still dragging that investigation out. That money was to come from the DNC when it actually was from the White House. I got a phone call in the first half of 1996 from Hillary saying that "Your Janet Reno said we already are going to be impeached. But we were going to win the election. This is a beautiful place to get back at our enemies!" How do you interpret this?

In response to CNBC, guest Watergate Bob Woodward's work in June of 1996, reveals foreign money from China coming into the White House. And G. Gordon Liddy's comment in the other matter that Hillary is up to her neck in it. Look at the pictures of Hillary right in there with the visits of Chinese to the White House. With this going on, I wrote in a letter to them that there is no one waving a red flag around here. I had, in previous months, said in two different correspondence to please not fall into the mistake that Nixon had made in the 1972 Campaign when he was a clear winner. But I may have been too late in the spring of 1996. It may have contributed to Hillary's daily calls each morning. She was playing and trying to get to me but they were playing with the election laws and the ones that define the taking of money from foreign governments. Violations were clear. They are masters at politics. Was the need for a large victory so great? Or the need for a mandate for their views that strong?

Now nineteen scholars give their view of what is impeachable and a definition of high crimes and misdemeanors. They reference the authors of the federalist papers, who emphasize that the power and responsibility of the President are awesome. And only a person with extraordinary integrity and the highest reputation for honesty and virtue could be trusted to bear it. The Democrats supporting experts lowered the standards to a near tyrant to stop before impeachment should be implemented.

Senator Specter floats the idea of curtailing the impeachment process and moving to a criminal trial after the President is out of office. Because there is no two-thirds majority in the Senate, he can be indicted and a judge can decide whether he should go to jail. Newt Gingrich resigned recently, but the President fights on. The administration's attempt and clear political maneuvering displayed themselves when it asked for some kind of "summary judgment." Without the hearing and testimony of witnesses being reviewed and heard by the House it is the duty of the Committee to review and investigate the indictments of perjury and obstruction of justice, including possible witness tampering. Do we just drop this without a criminal hearing on these charges also?

Conflicts in testimony from depositions exist. Why could he not have just told the truth in the depositions? We all knew he failed at covering up. Although we already heard their efforts clearly there would not have been as much pressure to impeach. If he waited until the August deposition to admit an inappropriate relationship, why make new false statements under oath? This is how Watergate developed, no way are we going to level with the public.

Bob Livingston, the speaker-to-be in the next Congress, said he would like this matter over before the new session began. But on MSNBC radio, he condemned Clinton in this matter, saying he has responsibility to the American people to live by the laws and obey them. He also pointed out there had been no reconciliation or admission of a behavior problem. In the negotiations with Paula Jones at this late date the White House is still in denial and trying to avoid an apology. It seems there is an underlying drive to try and pull things off even when telling the truth would be much better. It is part of Clinton's nature that dates back to their days in Arkansas.

On November 13, 1998, a Paula Jones settlement is reached for $850,000. Case closed. But Judge Wright may bring contempt charges against the President for statements made in court. On Monday November 16, 1996, impeachment in the House begins. The White House has not responded to the eighty-one questions. Ken Starr gives his purpose and conclusions to the House Committee. He is factual and refrains from concluding if the President's actions are impeachable, leaving that decision, as it should be, up to the members. Republicans ask questions to justify the investigation.

While Democrats never questioned the facts in the report they played some politics by questioning need of the report. Even if the results are not impeachable polls show by two-thirds that Starr received a favorable rating for his work.

It was debated that if there are not the votes in the House, should there be a censure or criminal trial after Clinton is out of office? Paula Jones says she no longer wants an apology. "He lied so much it would not mean a thing." It would be empty. It is safe to note all the years she asked for one. If Bill would had apologized, she would not have had much recourse. It would have been difficult to find attorneys who would have taken the case. The admission would have resolved the dispute and the monetary claim would have been hard to move forward. But they decided to fight the truth with deceit, denial and defiance. Justice has a way of coming around.

The Democrats must love the White House attorney and spokespeople saying the President did not lie or commit perjury at this point. They have to defend that publicly at this date. He has apologized for lying to the American public but still not addressed lying under oath in either the deposition or to the grand jury. It could follow him after office. The White House replies to the eighty-one questions with their long, evasive answers to yes/no questions. Janet Reno asked for an extension in Ickie's indictment to appoint special counsel. Hyde says this is the last chance for the White House to respond and that he intended to call Janet Reno and Louis Freed to testify about campaign finance and memos not yet turned over.

Even the people defending the White House seem to be unhappy. Their faces and tone show they don't like Bill Clinton, the man, anymore but are defending just his policies. He sent a letter with the response taking a sarcastic swipe at his accusers. Remember, he is now saying there was no perjury and apparently intends to fight until he gets off completely.

First of week hearings had testimony from individuals affected by perjury or who had committed perjury to demonstrate the implications of lying under oath. Some progress is made selling the seriousness of perjury and the White House is still saying the President did not commit perjury. And all you have is what Starr said. They respond by saying they would call in Monica Lewinsky and Linda Tripp to give testimony. The Democrats in the House are quick to counter that they want to move this along.

Bob Barr has been stating he thinks the President committed perjury and it rises to an impeachable offense. Gregory Craig is going to lead off, and he says there was no lying by the President. The arrogant responses to the eighty-one questions are beginning to hurt the White House, which is also pointing out that impeachment would be too much for the nature of the alleged offenses, while Hyde notes that no one is calling Monica a liar. But they still contend he did not lie under oath.

Bennett makes good points on a political talk show if it can't get through the Senate, a trial would be disruptive and the polls show most of the America public don't want the President impeached. And it is not bipartisan, so why push it. A response is how else can they show their disapproval of his abuse of office and lying to the American public.

On the first day Gregory Craig, the White House defense attorney gave his interpretation of the Jones deposition. The President was evasive, incomplete, misleading even maddening, but it was not perjury. Academics testify, intellectuals splitting hairs with the questions and answers that the President gave. Truth is usually yes or no. They keep putting us through intellectual arguments that they can only explain to us. They can even explain how Monica Lewinsky can have a sexual relationship with the President. But he claims he did not have one with her. He referred to this in his testimony as the President being the one disposed.

Both Democratic and Republicans give arguments but no one on the Committee changes position. Each member gets to gives a summary before their vote.

1. Perjury Grand Jury 21 I. 16 no

2. Perjury in Paula Jones, one less vote here than Grand Jury

3. Obstruction of Justice

There is an address from the White House as they vote directed at Congress and the American people in preparation for the vote the next week in the full House.

He acknowledges his own wrongdoing. "What I want the American people to know and what I want the Congress to know is that I am profoundly sorry for all I have done wrong, in words and deeds. I never of should mislead the country, the Congress, my friends and my family." He also will accept a censure.

The President and his defenders in the House are still not admitting any legal wrong, especially anything specific. They are saying the article of perjury and others are not specific enough. At the same time, he says he is sorry for what he has done.

The next day, the last article of impeachment passes committee.

4. Abuse of power

Some Democrats start to call for the President to resign. In Israel, Clinton responds that he will not resign. That does not enter into his thinking. He states that he did not commit perjury. "This is not a perjury case. I have no intentions of doing that."

The first day of this historic week, a few more Republicans who have been undecided commit their votes for impeachment. Even the White House is saying that now it looks like they have the votes to carry. Wednesday, one day before the scheduled debate in the full House on the articles of impeachment. The President receives a report from U.N. inspectors from Iraq and decides to launch an air attack. With earlier non compliances and the holy month about to begin, it would be disrespectful in that part of the world to start any action during that period. The President addresses the nation and explains the action at this time as necessary. Some suspect the timing but support the President's efforts. The House speaker delays the debate and takes up a resolution to ask for bipartisan support for the President's decision to attack and the personnel in the armed forces.

Republican leaders ask for a vote to resume on Friday even though the air attacks may not be over. Hillary says she thinks her husband is doing a good job and so do most Americans. She also says that the whole world thinks he is doing well, citing their recent visit to the Middle East. I know from her mother and sister when they start with that whole world, they're upset.

Besides the debate in the House, a lot of members are talking about slick Willy and how Bill has reneged on deals. There is a mistrust among politicians who don't accept the personal experiences with him where he misled them in dealings.

The Ford Building where additional evidence is available for Congress only, is not available to the public but some Republicans go, especially borderline members, after persuasion by the leadership. But Democrats decline to look at the additional evidence. Bob Livingston is in trouble having had to acknowledge he had offers during the course of his marriage. The Iraq campaign continues as Congress resumes its schedule. Some Democrats protest about not having the option to vote on censure but the Republican leadership says they are not here to debate censure but act on impeachment if censure is appropriate. It can occur in the Senate. The Saturday before the vote Hillary speaks to the Democrats and thanks them, pointing out how this is different from Nixon and Watergate. Then Livingston steps down, resigns and asks the President to do the same.

The Washington Post quotes J.C. Watts, "If our country looks the other way, our country will lose its way."

Democrats walk out just before the vote in protest but return.

Article	Y	N	Other
One	228	206	1 carries perjury
Two	205	229	1
Three	221	212	2 carries obstruction of justice
Four	148	285	2

Hyde comments that there is enough evidence for a trial in the Senate. The President holds a gathering at the White House. Over 100 Democratic members attend. Everyone at the White House has a smile on their face. He asks the American people to join him and move forward. But where are the other Democrats? His polls do go up. Perhaps the American public considers some kind of censure appropriate and are now saying it's enough and want to move forward. This display of defiance receives considerable criticism in the following weeks, however. Former Presidents Ford and Carter propose a censure that would include admission that Bill lied under oath. But the process is now over in the Senate.

VIII. The Senate Trial

The Trial of the President in the Senate begins with the foregone conclusion that the neccessary 67 votes are not obtainable.

White House supporters are raising the question that since it was a lame duck Congress and not the new Congress that voted, somehow the impeachment was invalid, that it will not go over. As Congress is considered a continuing body, many are calling for a censure. Senator Byrd announces that people from the White House should stay out and it is up to the Senate now, while Al Gore publicly states the President did not lie. And Senators Byrd and Moynihand apparently are trying to draft a censure on paper.

Over the holidays, Senator Lott suggests calling an early vote and moves for censure but Hyde responds that they should consider their duty and not speed.

By January 4, 1999, a temporary procedure is worked out:

1. House managers, including Hyde, present case.

2. President's lawyers defend.

3. Senators submit questions.

4. Vote to dismiss and call witnesses at a later date with possibility of some form of censure.

It leaves out a full trial, and no witnesses. The House looks bad that the Senate treated it so lightly. Also, the exist that the White House will not admit guilt to the two articles and there is not enough time to present evidence of guilt or innocence. How can they censure if the White House will only stipulate guilt in a censure resolution? But we are going to claim we are free of charges. Obviously, most senators and others would like to have this resolved quickly but it leaves too many open questions and does not address their obligation to constitutional duty. Discussion continues on whether to call witnesses and abandon the idea of a short four-day trial. Conservatives want the right to call witnesses and the White House could call their own without the procedures worked out, Majority Leader Lott announces the trial will begin on Thursday.

Cregory Craig, the President's counsel, says that the case against the President is legally and factually deficient. The White House is posturing on how they are going to try and prove innocence on the facts. The 106th Senate opens. The House impeachment managers request an option to call witnesses and Lott announces it looks like there will be a full trial. Then, on January 7, 1999, the senators take their oath as impartial jurors and the articles of impeachment are presented by Hyde.

Lott announces that they will all convene in the old Senate Building to work out a procedure. The White House states that it will stipulate the facts in Starr's report if no witnesses are called. But apparently, they will contest the interpretation of fact, continuing to claim that the President is innocent, but for the purposes of Senate trial they are willing not to contest them. But they want to maintain the right to contest the facts in the future. The White House says if they do call witnesses they will fight all the way. Witnesses would cause the facts to be re-lived and it would look bad for the White House going through a point by point it would also humanize the matter. It could only hurt the White House case. Both sides seem to be worried about Monica and how that would appear she would be a necessary witness for the perjury and to counter the President's claim that he did not touch her. His defense against perjury is that he was deposed during sex and basically she had sex with him but he did not touch her in any sexual manner.

What is also important is that the Democrats complained in the House that witnesses were not called but now are insisting on no witness here. It was because of the time constraint and both parties supported a expedient hearing that would end before Christmas.

Julie Steel, on January 7, 1999, is charged with three counts of obstruction of justice and one count of perjury. She backed the Kathleen Willey story, then contested it. The decision was handed down by Starr today.

In the historic old Senate chambers, with all senators present, all agree on trial procedures, a bipartisan agreement in private.

Opening motions are to begin on Wednesday.

Twenty-four hours for the House managers.

Twenty-four for the President's defense. Sixteen hours of questions from Senators.

But this puts off whether witnesses are to be called with Democrats giving up demands for no witnesses. Witnesses would be interviewed in private and under oath. If they are to be called, the full Senate would have to vote.

Possible witnesses: Monica Lewinsky, Betty Currie and Vernon Jordan. Monica Lewinsky's statement conflicts with the White House claims. No one is questioning that she told the truth in her Grand Jury testimony and perhaps there is more she has not addressed. She also signed an affidavit lying in the Paula Jones case prepared by the

White House. Betty could go over how the President had instructed her to say she did not know or see anything, including the retrieval of the gifts. Vernon Jordan is involved in finding a job for Lewinsky for her silence.

Then Podesta, Blumenthal and Dick Morris testify to establish that, early on, a coverup and suppression of the truth came from the President. Finally there is the possibility that some of the five women in the Paula Jones case could be called in if they want to establish that they were put under pressure to lie or remain silent to corroborate existing obstruction of justice testimony. Then the White House prepares a response on paper. They are saying a vote on each of the two articles is unfair, that the charges should be broken out and voted on separately. For each specific claim followed on January 12th with the $850,000 settlement to Paula Jones from Bill Clinton.

The White House releases a 130-page brief that the President is innocent, a challenge of the facts in the House case. The President plans to give his State of the Union address in one week, the day his defense begins. Trent Lott says they may want to call Kathleen Willey to testify. If the White House is questioning the facts now, then there is a need to call witness.

January 14, 1999, is the first day of the prosecution's case focused on the presentation of facts and the need to call witnesses. But do they persuade anyone?

Opening statement of Henry Hyde:

He opens with: "We are brought together on this solemn and historic occasion to perform important duties assigned to us by the Constitution. And speak on the importance of an oath."

Then he introduces the twelve other members of the House management team.

A. James Sensenbrenner

He starts off by quoting Theodore Roosevelt. "No, man is above the law and no man is below it, nor do we ask any man's permission when we require him to obey it. Obedience to the law is demanded as a right, not asked as a favor."

Sensenbrenner states that "The evidence will clearly show that President Clinton's false testimony to the Grand Jury was not a single or isolated instance which could be excused as a mistake, but rather a comprehensive and calculated plan to prevent the Grand Jury from getting the accurate testimony in order to do its job."

He cites the case of Judge Nixon who was removed for two count of perjury the votes 89 to 8 and 78 to 19. He claims the truth is the truth and a lie is a lie. There cannot be different levels of the truth for judges and for presidents.

Further, the evidence will show the President made other false statements to the Grand Jury regarding the nature and details of his relationship with Ms. Lewinsky at times when he did not refer to his prepared statement.

Second, the evidence will show that the President piled perjury upon perjury when he provided perjurious, false and misleading testimony to the Grand Jury concerning prior perjurious, false and misleading testimony given in the Paula Jones case.

Third he pointed out the filing of the false affidavit by his attorney in the Paula Jones case.

Fourth, the evidence will show that the President provided perjurious, false and misleading testimony to the

Grand Jury concerning his corrupt efforts to influence the testimony of witnesses and to impede the discovery of evidence in the Paula Jones civil rights action.

Finally, the President made perjurious, false and misleading statements to aides regarding his relationship with Ms. Lewinsky. In his Grand Jury testimony, the President tried to have it both ways on this issue. He testified that his statements to aides were both true and misleading--true and misleading. He then introduces Article II of impeachment obstruction of justice, and gives an overview of its various aspects as they relate to this case. They will be picked up by the House managers that follow in detail.

The President engaged in a conspiracy of crimes to prevent justice from being served. These are impeachable offenses for which the President should be convicted.

B. Ed Bryant

1. Responding in part to the Impeachment Article I, the President persists in a wrongheaded fashion with his legal hairsplitting of the term "sexual relations", which permits him to define that term in such a way that in the particular salacious act we are talking about here, one person has sex and the other person does not.

2. Responding to both articles of impeachment the President now would have you believe that he "was not focusing" when his attorney, Bob Bennett, was objecting during the deposition and attempting to cut off a very important line of questioning of the President by representing to Judge Wright that Ms. Lewinsky's affidavit proved that there was no need to go into this testimony about the President's life. He said that this affidavit proves that "there is absolutely no sex of any kind, in any manner, shape or form."

3. In his further response to Article I, the President effectively admits to being guilty of obstruction. As I read this, his pleading refers to the President himself, and he states that he, the President, "truthfully explained to the Grand Jury his efforts to answer the questions in the Jones deposition without disclosing his relationship with Ms. Lewinsky." So he claims he did answer the questions in the Jones deposition in a way so as not to disclose his relationship with Ms. Lewinsky.

4. In Bryant's address to Article II, the President denies that he encouraged Monica Lewinsky to submit a false affidavit in the Jones case.

5. In an additional response to Article II, the President asserts that "he believed that Ms. Lewinsky could have filed a limited and truthful affidavit that might have enabled her to avoid having to testify in the Jones case." That is an incredible statement. Bryant concludes that to resolve these discrepancies witnesses need to be called.

C. Asa Hutchinson

He addresses Article II, obstruction of justice, which he says, occurred first.

"As I said, it began on Friday, December 5th, when the witness list came from the Paula Jones case. Shortly thereafter, the President learned that the list included Monica Lewinsky."

But to compound the problem, less than a week later, On December 11, Judge Wright, Federal District Judge in Arkansas. Issued an order and that order directed that the President had to answer questions concerning other relationships that he might have had during a particular time frame with any state or federal employee.

Now, what happened during the time between when the President learned Monica Lewinsky was on the list and when he notified her of that fact on December 17 is very important. The President, during that time frame, talked to his friend, his confidant and his problem solver, Vernon Jordan. Mr. Jordan had come to the President's rescue on previous occasions and he was instrumental in securing consulting contracts for Mr. Webb Hubbell while Mr. Hubbell was under investigation by the independent counsel. (Vernon Jordan introduced Mr. Hubbell to the "right people" then and he received $100,000 just before resigning from the Justice Department.)

Then, he references Mr. Jordan's March 3, 1998, Grand Jury testimony.

"I am certain after the 11th that I had a conversation with the President and as part of that conversation I said to him that Betty Currie had called me about Monica Lewinsky. And the conversation was that he knew about her situation which was that she was pushed out of the White House, that she wanted to go to New York and he thanked me for helping her."

Then he points out Mr. Jordan's June 9, 1998, Grand Jury testimony in response as to why Vernon Jordan was contacting the White House about the status of Monica Lewinsky's lawyer. "The President asked me to get Monica Lewinsky a job. I got her a lawyer. The Drudge Report is out and she has a new counsel. I thought that was information that they ought to have." In the same June 9, 1998, testimony he points out another V. Jordan response.

"Information. He knew that I had gotten her a job, he knew that I had gotten her a lawyer. Information. He was interested in this matter. He is the source of it coming to my attention in the first place."

The presentation continues with: What happened? Things happened. He did, he made things happen, Monica Lewinsky got a job. The affidavit was signed and the President was informed by Mr. Jordan, through Betty Currie, that the mission was accomplished. The President said he had seen the witness list in the case and her name was on it. Ms. Lewinsky asked what she should do if subpoenaed, and the President responded, "Well, maybe you can sign an affidavit."

The House manager points out the President told Monica Lewinsky what she could say in order to hide their affair. "You know, you can always say you were coming to see Betty or that you were bringing me letters."

It should also be remembered that the President, when questioned about encouraging Monica Lewinsky to lie, denied these allegations, and therefore there is certainly a conflict in the testimony.

Then he presents what he told Betty Currie to say if questioned. First, "I was never really alone with Monica, right?"

Second, "You were always there when Monica was there, right?" "Monica came on to me, and I never touched her, right?"

He points out the President claims in his testimony that these statements to Betty were to refresh her own testimony, but then argues to the contrary.

This was not an attempt by the President to refresh his recollection. It was witness tampering, pure and simple.

Then he references Betty Currie's sworn testimony that the President called her a few days later to go over the same five points.

And this needs to be emphasized. Not only was witness coaching taking place on Sunday, but it took place a couple of days later. It was twice repeated by the President to Betty Currie. He needed to have her in line.

In order to carry out this coverup and obstruction, the President needed to go further. He needed not only for Betty Currie to repeat his false statements, but also for other witnesses, who would assuredly be called before the Federal Grand Jury and questioned by the news media in public forums, to do so.

And this brings us to the false statements that the President made to his White House staff and presidential aides. Let's call Sidney Blumenthal and John Podesta to the witness stand.

D. James Rogan

He addresses Article I, perjury, and presents the definition of sexual relationship approved by Judge Wright.

Definition of sexual relationship: "For the purposes of that deposition, a person engages in sexual relations when the person knowingly engages in or causes contact with the [certain enumerated body parts] of any person with an intent to arouse or gratify the sexual desire of any person."

Rogan then told how the President misled and lied in his answers regarding his sexual relationship with Monica and followed up with lying to the American public.

So by the time the President sat down for his Grand Jury testimony to answer these questions under oath, he had put himself in a huge box. He could not continue the outright lie because Ms. Lewinsky had turned over her blue dress for DNA testing, and at the time of his Grand Jury testimony he didn't know what the results would be of that FBI test. Under such circumstances, continuing the lie was too risky a strategy even for the most accomplished of gamblers. But if he told the truth, his earlier perjury and obstruction of justice would have ended his presidency. He felt sure he would have been driven from office.

He then referenced how the President had Dick Morris take a poll. The results showed the public would forgive him for an adultery but not for perjury and obstruction of justice. The President then told Dick Morris, "We'll just have to win." Rogan moves on to August 17, and presents the statement used by the President to respond to some of the question concerning Monica Lewinsky and their relationship.

A. When I was alone with Ms. Lewinsky on certain occasions in early 1996 and once in early 1997, I engaged in conduct that was wrong. These encounters did not consist of sexual intercourse. They did not constitute sexual relations as I understood that term to be defined at the January 17, 1998, deposition but they did involve inappropriate intimate contact.

(Sounds like he wants it both ways)

The President used that prepared statement as a substitute answer for specific questions about his conduct with Ms. Lewinsky nineteen separate times during his testimony before the Grand Jury.

The evidence shows the President used this prepared statement in order to justify the perjurious answers he gave at his deposition that were intended to affect the outcome of the Paula Jones case. He points out that the statement was given in 1996 at the beginning of the relationship. Now she is no longer a twenty one year-old intern but a paid employee of the White House. But it was on November 15, 1995.

In fact, she testified that the first time she ever spoke to the President was on November 15, 1995, during the government shutdown. And she said that the very first time that she ever spoke to the President was the same day he invited her back to the Oval Office and began a sexual relationship with her.

He points out confusing and evasive answers to the questions in the Grand Jury by the President as to what the President understood the definition to be.

A. The person being deposed. If the person being deposed contacted those parts of another person's body with an intent to arouse or gratify, that was covered.

What the President now was saying to the Grand Jury is that during their intimate relationship in the Oval Office, Monica Lewinsky had sexual relations with him, but he didn't have sexual relations with her.

Rogan then cites another similar evasive response.

Q. Your--that statement is a completely false statement. Whether or not Mr. Bennett knew of your relationship with Ms. Lewinsky, the statement that there was "no sex of any kind in any manner, shape or form with President Clinton" was an utterly false statement. Is that correct?

A. It depends upon what the meaning of the word "is" means. If "is" means is, and never has been, that's one thing. If it means, there is none, that was a completely true statement. Rogan gives another example of perjury. That could be cleared up with other conflicts in testimony by calling witnesses.

Question to the President:

After you gave her the gifts on December 28, did you speak with your secretary, Ms. Currie, and ask her to pick up a box of gifts that were some compilation of gifts that Ms. Lewinsky would have---

Answer: No, sir, I didn't do that.

Question: to give to Ms. Currie?

Answer: I did not do that.

The consensus at this point is that if the White House does not contest this they may be found guilty of the two articles but removal from office will fail. And a point-by-point contesting of these facts would lead to witnesses being called and possible trouble.

Friday, the next day he makes an argument that if you compare Monica's statement to Bill's you have to conclude Bill committed perjury and you have to challenge those who don't believe to allow them to call Monica Lewinsky and other witnesses like Vernon Jordan and Betty Currie to clearly demonstrate who is telling the truth and how Paula Jones's rights to a fair trial and access to the truth had been denied.

It is a lie in the Grand Jury testimony by the President when he said he tried to be truthful with his testimony in the Paula Jones deposition. So the false statements in that deposition must also be considered when making their determinations.

Point by each of the House managers:

A. Bill McCollum

He expresses he has no personal animosity toward our President, then states that he happens to believe that, if the President--if any President--commits the crimes of perjury, obstruction of justice and witness tampering, he should not be allowed to remain in office, for if he is allowed to do so, it would undermine our courts and our system of justice.

B. George Gekas

He talks about how it is a matter of the President trying to destroy the rights of a fellow American citizen. "This is what the gravamen of all that has occurred up to now really is." This goes beyond saying "This is just about sex." And we must look at the consequence of this perjury and obstruction of justice.

He asked them to look at the deposition a month earlier on December 23, 1997. When the President was asked if he had ever had sexual relations with anyone other than his wife while he was governor or president. His answer was no. This, he points out, was the start of what led to an explosion of falsehoods in the August 1998 Grand Jury.

C. Steve Chabot

On the law, he explains that there are four parts to perjury the oath, intent, falsity and materiality. In this case the oath was proper. And intent requires that the false testimony was knowingly stated and described. Mr. Chabot points out that the Presidents own attorney willfully misled the court.

"I have no doubt that he walked up to a line that thought he understood reasonable people--and you maybe have reached this conclusion--could determine that he crossed over that line and that what for him was truthful but misleading or non-responsive and misleading or evasive was in fact false."

His own attorneys admit that he had instructed others to give false testimony as with Betty Currie, who was also used to demonstrate intent. As to false statements, he referenced the evidence his colleagues had already presented.

As to the final matter of materiality, Chabot cites the Supreme Court in Kungys v. United States, saying it is simply whether it had a "natural tendency to influence" or was "capable of influencing" the official proceeding. Chabot closes by saying "We will be sending a message to our children, to my children, that telling the truth doesn't really matter if you have a good lawyer or you are an exceptionally skilled liar." And that "no person is above the law and that this great nation remains an entity governed by the rule of law."

D. Christopher Cannon:

On obstruction of justice he points out it is not necessary for a defendant to succeed in obstructing justice but simply to attempt to is sufficient to violate the statute. And that the intent to act corruptly can be inferred from that proof that the defendant knew corrupt actions would obstruct the justice being administered.

E. Bob Barr:

He addresses the point that Ms. Lewinsky testified under oath before the Grand Jury that the scheme to file this false affidavit was devised or hatched during a telephone conversation with the President on December 17, 1997, a call the President initiated to Ms. Lewinsky at 2 or 2:30 a.m. Then he cited how they had heard, in an early presentations the President's lawyer, Mr. Robert Bennett, state in court directly to Judge Wright when he presented the false affidavit, "There is absolutely no sex of any kind in any manner, shape or form," and that the President was "fully aware of Ms. Lewinsky's affidavit."

Later in the deposition, when Mr. Bennett read to the President the portion of the affidavit in which Ms. Lewinsky denies their relationship and asked him, "Is that a true and accurate statement as far as you know it?", the President answered, "That is absolutely true." This statement is neither credible nor true. It is perjury.

With regard to the issue of perjury before the Grand Jury concerning the affidavit, we as managers would show that, when asked before the Grand Jury whether he had instructed Ms. Lewinsky to file a truthful affidavit, President Clinton testified, "Did I hope she would be able to get out of testifying on an affidavit? Absolutely. Did I want her to execute a false affidavit? No. I did not."

Then he referenced the coaching of Ms. Currie on Sunday, January 18, 1998. I will only emphasize that it was at that time and in that way, in that manner that the President led Ms. Currie through a series of statements and determinate questions to establish a set of facts describing his relationship with Ms. Lewinsky at the White House that supported his false testimony.

On December 19, 1997, Ms. Lewinsky was served with a subpoena in the Jones case requiring her to produce each and every gift given to her by the President. Then, on December 28, Ms. Lewinsky again met with the President in the Oval Office, at which time they exchanged gifts. They also discussed the fact that the lawyers in the Jones case had subpoenaed all the President's gifts to Mrs. Lewinsky and especially a hat pin. During that conversation, Ms. Lewinsky asked the President whether she removed the gifts from her house or gave them to someone, maybe Betty. At that time, according to Ms. Lewinsky's sworn testimony, the President responded, "Let me think about that." Barr goes on to point out that later that same day, Betty Currie drove to Ms. Lewinsky's apartment to pick up the gifts and how this constitutes withholding of evidence. Barr walks us through the job search by Vernon Jordan once it is clear Monica is likely to be called as a witness in the Jones case. He states that this aspect of the case against the President is extremely important. She gets the job, but what does the President get? The key is an affidavit to throw the Jones lawyers off the trail and possibly obtain a witness outside the practical reach of the attorneys, much like the absent witnesses we have seen in large numbers in the campaign financing investigations.

Now this is obstruction of justice and witness tampering. Then he references the President's attorney, Mr. Bennett, and how on September 30, 1998, long after the truth came out he wrote Judge Wright about how she should not rely upon the statements made during the deposition because parts of the affidavit were "misleading and not true." Sounds like perjury.

Stephen Buyer: Constitutional Basis.

Buyer points out how President Clinton violated his constitutional oath to "preserve, protect and defend the Constitution of the United States" and constitutional duty to "take care the laws be faithfully executed." Then Buyer points out the President can be removed from office on impeachment for and conviction of treason, bribery, or other high crimes and misdemeanors. With perjury and obstruction of justice fit as "other high crimes." Perjury and bribery are side by side.

While we have been discussing how perjury and obstruction of justice are attacks on our judicial system, we must recognize how the judicial system is a core function of the government. When Mr. Manager Henry Hyde speaks of the rule of law protecting us from the knock on the door at 3 a.m., what exactly was he referring to? Well, in totalitarian societies, rulers may drag the ruled off to prison at any time for any reason. Our system differs because we require our leaders to go through a judicial procedure before they put someone in prison or otherwise violate their individual rights.

Before Buyer closes he points out how no one in the military would have the privilege to serve any more if they had committed the same acts or broken the same laws. "Equal justice under law"--that principle so embodies the American constitutional order that we have it carved in stone on the front of the Supreme Court building right across the street.

Lindsey Graham: Precedents for Impeachment.

He makes a passionate argument that the President be removed. Graham points out that the Supreme Court said nine to zero -- a shutout legally--"Mr. President, you will stand subject to this suit."

Referring to the Paula Jones case, Graham states that when he chose to lie, when he chose to manipulate the evidence of witnesses against him and get his friends to go lie for him, he, in fact, I think, vetoed that decision.

But, ladies and gentlemen, what he stands charged of in the Senate happened eight months later after some members of this body said, "Mr. President, square yourself by the law. Mr. President, if you go into that Federal Grand Jury and you lie again, you're risking your presidency." Graham finishes with several examples of judges who were removed for perjury, and makes a call for witnesses so that each side can present a full case in order for them to resolve this matter.

One could not live with oneself, knowing that you were going to leave a perjury as a judge on the bench.

Charles Canady: Academic Historical Foundation for High Crimes and Misdemeanors Removal.

Canady argues for the removal of the President offering the comments of Senator Al Gore on Judge Chailorne in 1986:

"It is incumbent upon the Senate to fulfill its constitutional responsibility and strip this man of his title. An individual who has knowingly falsified tax returns has no business receiving a salary derived from the tax dollars of honest citizens."

Canady disputes the President's attorneys that his offenses, felonies, do not rise to the level of "High Crimes and Misdemeanors."

Perjury and obstruction of justice, I summit to you, clearly "undermine the integrity of office." I ask you if these offenses do not undermine the office, what offenses would?

Canady points out that the removal power is not just when the immediate destruction of our institutions is threatened. On the contrary, the removal power should be understood as a positive grant of authority to the Senate to preserve, protect and strengthen our constitutional system against the misconduct of federal officials when that misconduct would subvert, undermine or weaken the institution of our government.

Canady finishes by warning of setting one standard for the removal of judges and another for the President and asks the Senate to considers removal of President William Jefferson Clinton.

They take a lunch break during which Senator Hatch speaks to the media. Out of courtesy he invites the President to clarify and clear up ambiguities and goes on to say that others who have suggested asking the President to testify are partisan and being political.

George Gekas: Summation.

Gekas speaks to how this is a case of truth and fairness.

"In the words of our colleagues who made magnificent presentations of the facts and law to you, the words 'truth' and 'fairness' were some of the strongest and most profound that we heard in various degrees in touching upon various subjects that were important to our presentation."

Hyde: Closes the House managers' case.

"It's not even a question of lying about sex. The matter before this body is a question of lying under oath. This is a public act. The matter before you is a question of the willful, premeditated, deliberate corruption of the nation's system of justice through perjury and obstruction of justice."

The White House is uncomfortable with the long break before they present their defense because it will give people and the Senators time to discuss the prosecution side.

Presentation of the President's Defense Mr. Ruff: President's counsel opens:

"William Jefferson Clinton is not guilty of the charges that have been preferred against him. He did not commit perjury, he did not obstruct justice, he must not be removed from office."

Mr. Ruff points out that judges who are appointed for life are different from the President, who is elected ever four years.

Then Mr. Ruff also points out that the recollection of two witnesses may differ and references the Supreme Court.

"Equally honest witnesses may well have different recollection of the same event, and thus, a conviction for perjury ought not to rest entirely upon an oath against an oath."

Then Mr. Ruff states:

Now, to conclude that the President lied to the Grand Jury about his relationship with Ms. Lewinsky, you must determine--forgive me--that he touched certain parts of her body, but for proof you have her oath against his oath.

Mr. Ruff moves on to the false affidavit he had his attorney, Mr. Bennett, submit in the Paula Jones case so he would not have to answer any questions about a sexual relationship with Ms. Lewinsky. He contends the President was not aware of what was going on as the President claims and that the videotape is misinterpreted.

In reference to Betty Currie, he points out what the President said to her when he found out she was going in front of the Grand Jury. "I didn't want her to be untruthful to the Grand Jury. And if her memory was different than mine, it was fine, just go in there and tell them what she thought."

He makes a good presentation and the arrogance of the President's counsel displayed in the House Judiciary Committee is missing.

State Of The Union:
Clinton gives a good speech, as he can. As he said, the Union is strong. The economy and budget are in good condition. It is a culmination of polls as to what the American public wants over some seventy-five points.

Gregory Graig: On Perjury.

Graig claims the articles of impeachment are not specific enough. He also claims the House managers tried to confuse lying about being alone with Ms. Lewinsky in the Paula Jones deposition and the President Grand Jury testimony. He then says there is no "direct lie" in the President's testimony that is perjurious. Graig says making a point about it being 1995 or 1996 when the relationship with Ms. Lewinsky started is immaterial. She was an intern and then became a government employee. It did not change the relationship, just her title. But Ms. Lewinsky going from young intern to full federal employee could also be another example of reward for sex.

Graig makes the argument that the President used his own definition of sex that the President had in mind, (intercourse) as in the Paula Jones case. Not the definition agreed to "sexual relations" that the Jones attorney defined as to (touch specific part of the body to gratify sexually the other party) when answering questions, even though they discussed and agreed to the definition. Graig states to contend that he was committing perjury when he told the Grand Jury that he genuinely believed his interpretation of the definition--that is just speculation about what is in his mind and it is not the stuff or fuel of a perjury prosecution.

Not answering questions about touching specific body parts or admitting a sexual relation is one of the major perjury charges in this case. To explain away sexual contact that leads to orgasm as not being a sexual relationship. And to accept his prepared statement just having an "inappropriate intimate contact" that he referred to over and over again as his answer to the questions in the Grand Jury. To get him out of any legal problems from answering questions whether there was a sexual relation with Monica Lewinsky. In both the Paula Jones case and the Grand Jury is up there with oral sex is not sex and what the definition of is is. The President is obviously concerned and his attorney has probably advised him that he is at risk of criminal charges being brought against him.

Graig: Will have you look so closely at some of the individual elements (each detail on its own), you can't see the big picture.

The prosecutors would like you to take a step back and look at the totality (over all picture) and see the well-planned lying and witness tampering.

Cheryl Mills: Obstruction of Justice.

Mills contends the President was just trying to continue the coverup of an embarrassing illicit affair not trying to obstruct justice in concealing his relationship with Ms. Lewinsky. She also contends it was only Ms. Lewinsky's idea and action involving the retrieval of gifts that ended up under Betty Currie's bed.

Mills, in response to the President's coaching of Betty Currie on what to remember. She says there was no obstruction of justice because there was no threat or intimidation associated with it. She also questions the House managers where they claim the President's "intent" was to influence her testimony. She was not a likely witness in the Jones case, even though she, more than any one else besides Monica or the President, knew firsthand of their relationship.

Mills concludes that she is not worried about Paula Jones's civil rights. Because Judge Wright determined after considering all the facts we have here and the law that there was no case against the President. It was dismissed on "summary judgement" and that was pending appeal before being settled privately.

David Kendall: Defense.

Kendall addressed the five remaining points in the obstruction case. He starts with the President, asking Ms. Lewinsky to sign an affidavit. "Neither the President or

Jordan ever told Lewinsky that she had to lie." They did not tell her to tell the truth and it was implied and suggested as a way to get out of testifying in the Paula Jones case.

Kendall then dismisses the claim that the President and Lewinsky, in a late night December 17 phone call after the President knew she was on the witness list, talked about what she could and could not say. "You know, you can always say you were coming to see Betty or that you were bringing me letters." It was usual cover talk whenever they discussed their relationship.

Kendall argues the President simply was not focusing when Mr. Bennett, the President's lawyer, states that according to the affidavit, "there is no sex of any kind in any manner, shape or form." And that Mr. Bennett's recent letter to the judge apologizing for the false affidavit is not an admission of wrong.

Then Kendall argues that the President's telling his staff and others that there was no relationship is not relevant because they were never called or would be called as witnesses in the Paula Jones case.

Finally, on the issue of a job for silence he simply said there was no quid pro quo. Even though she sought a job for her efforts, including signing the false affidavit as the Tripp tapes demonstrate as well as the evidence of the days before and after she received the subpoena in the Jones case. They demonstrated a frantic effort to get her a job out of town, out of reach of the Paula Jones attorneys and a false affidavit worded just right to please Vernon Jordan, thus avoiding her testifying.

Dale Bumpers: Character Defense.

He speaks to how fine a people the Clintons are and what anguish this matter has brought them. He is a long-time friend and former Senator.

Next the questions from the senators. Most are designed to bolster a thier position whether they are supportive of the prosecution or part of the President's defense. Senator Byrd asks them to consider a vote to dismiss on grounds that there is not a two-thirds majority in favor of removing. Such a motion is scheduled soon as part of the procedure already worked out. The question of witnesses is the main thrust of the House prosecutors. They say they need them to move this case forward and that they and the President are the ones who could clear up the disputed areas.

Monica is back in Washington. The House used Ken Starr's ability to question her as part of her immunity deal. Although she has been questioned over twenty times on this matter. It is the first chance the House managers have to meet with her and evaluate her as a possible witness to bolster their case.

The following session opened up with a few questions, then a motion to dismiss from Democrat Senator Byrd. Another vote was then taken to move it behind closed doors in order to work out the differences. The White House is concerned that it may take two votes one on whether the President is guilty of the articles and a second to see if he should be removed. They are also refusing to answer a new list of ten questions sent by Republicans to the President. Trent Lott the next day: "Maybe we need some way to convince but not remove." They work out a short list of witnesses: M. Lewinsky, V. Jordan and S. Blumenthal.

Meantime with Hubbell:

A District of Columbia Appeals Court ruled that Starr is justified in bringing charges of tax fraud/evasion against Hubbell, his wife and his tax lawyer even though most of the evidence came from Hubbell's own documents. The money in question, over $700,000 is believed to be hush money from Clinton friends for Hubbell in the Whitewater matter.

The next day the first vote is on a motion to dismiss, then a vote on the witnesses forty-four for dismissal of the articles fails. This is a block of votes that the White House wants to hold onto if they can keep them in their camp. They can stop removal from office.

Vote for witnesses carries.

Depositions will be taken through Sunday to expedite the process, with the questions limited to disputed facts even with these two partisan votes. Both Lott and Daschle expressed their desire for an expeditious conclusion with a bipartisan end to the trial. Then both Republican and Democratic senators try to work out a way to depose the three witnesses by Monday. On Friday the Senate took a break and the three subpoenas for witnesses went out. Some Republicans push for a vote on the facts so that they can vote against removal. Some Democrats would go along with this, but not all Republicans. Senator Hatch responds to complaints about calling Monica.

They are not concerned about Monica Lewinsky. "If that dress hadn't been in existence, Monica Lewinsky would have been ruined. They would have slandered and smeared her right into ground. They would of thrashed her, like they tried to do to Paula Jones."

The President's press secretary, Joe Lockhart, comments on the Republicans calling witness. "There is an attempt here by the Republican majority. To play out this process, in a way that can inflict the maximum political damage on the President."

In the next three days Monica Lewinsky, Vernon Jordan and Sidney Blumenthal testified respectfully. Monica Lewinsky was businesslike and did not come across as the venerable victim of Clinton that the House managers had hoped for. She did not say the President told her to lie or sign a false affidavit but her testimony makes it clear she was never asked to be truthful either.

Bryant: In fact, you did deny the relationship to the Jones lawyers in the affidavit that you signed under penalty of perjury, is that right?

Lewinsky: I denied a sexual relationship.

Bryant: The President did not, in that conversation on December 17, 1997, or any other conversation for that matter, instruct you to tell the truth, is that correct?

Lewinsky: That's correct.

Vernon Jordan testified that he got Monica a job at the request of the President, but it was not for her silence. He admits to talking to Ms. Lewinsky about a note she had written to the President but denies asking her to "go home and make sure they're not there," as Lewinsky claims.

Sidney Blumenthal was the last to testify. The House managers were trying to make a case that he was lied to about Monica because he was a potential witness.

Rogan: What did the President tell you?

Blumenthal: "He spoke, uh, fairly rapidly, as I recall, at that point and said that she had come on to him and made a demand for sex. That he had rebuffed her, turned her down, and that she, uh, threatened him....He said that she said to him, uh, that she was called "the stalker" by her peers and that she hated the term, and that she would claim that they had an affair whether they had or they hadn't and that she would tell people." This is another example of how far they will go to lie and turn the truth around. This is also demonstrates Bill and Hillary's old tactic of trashing people to hide the truth.

Friday was a day off for the Senate, with the trial resuming on Saturday. When the House managers would present the new testimony and restate their case followed by the White House defense. The misconduct and the claim that harm was done to the justice system wasn't strong enough to remove the President. They did not make a case that the framers would have believed was truly dangerous to the state.

Sunday came with the possible vote on the facts dead as some refer to it as a simple majority instead of two-thirds to convict. More talk of a strong censure begins. Will these Democrats be voicing the need for a censure as they are now and had in the past. Once the vote on the two articles was over? Senior Senator Byrd said he believed that the charges rose to the level of high crimes and misdemeanors but the question was would it be in the best interest of the nation to remove the President.

Monday was the final day of presentations. The closing arguments were quite similar to the opening ones with the House managers restating their conviction and asking the senators to weigh the principles, not the polls. Henry Hyde closes with "And now let us all take our place in history on the side of honor and, oh, yes, let right be done." Next, Ruff concludes with the President's defense taking little of the allotted time. He restates how the President did not commit perjury or obstruct justice and should not be removed.

Tuesday is the start of a three-day, closed-door deliberation (most jury deliberations are private), with each Senator entering a fifteen-minute reason on the record for their vote. The vote was fifty-nine to forty-one, short of sixty-seven to hold the debate on the Senate floor. By Wednesday, a few Republicans announced they would not vote for one or both of the articles. Whether a simple majority for conviction might be reached is in jeopardy. On Thursday a report in the New York Times states that the President has vowed to get back at the Republicans who brought this on in the next election. The White House denies the President has apparently told this to his top aides.

At noon on January 12, 1999, the vote on both articles of impeachment is taken.

	Guilty	Not	
Article I	45	55	Perjury
Article II	50	50	Obstruction

From the White House the President addresses his acquittal:

"Now that Senate has fulfilled its constitutional responsibility, bringing this process to a conclusion, I want to say again to the American people how profoundly sorry I am for what I said and did to trigger these events and the great burden they have imposed on the Congress and the American people."

He concludes that this can be and must be a time of reconciliation and renewal for America.

Press: In your heart, sir, can you forgive and forget?

Clinton: I believe any person who asks for forgiveness has to be prepared to give it. The constitutional process is over. The wisdom of the architects of the Constitution is apparent. They defined a simple majority to impeach but created a two-thirds barrier to remove in the Senate. The two Houses are split, like the American public, with most giving William Jefferson Clinton support for his policies but three-fourths believing he lied under oath.

IX. Janet Reno Hiding The Truth

Janet Reno had a reputation as a tough prosecutor as Dade County's State Attorney in Miami, Florida, before becoming the Clinton administration's Attorney General in 1993.

There are some disturbing cases she was involved in as State Attorney where the truth was not the objective. Was political ambition her motive? Bobby Fijnje, a 12-year-old at the time, was charged and held for two years in a juvenile detention center before a jury cleared him. He refused a plea bargain. Grant Snowden, a police officer whose wife ran a daycare center in his home and who had been tried and proved his innocence once, was charged again and convicted, spending 12years in person before winning on appeal. In both of these cases, the only or primary evidence was testimony from children who had been misled by child psychologists brought in by the State Attorney's Office specifically for their program. Police and social workers had been removed from the process to reduce the trauma to the children and their parents. The methods used to get false testimony from the children revealed a repulsive disregard for the children's welfare. They had them pretend they were being molested and asked them repeated questions about what that would be like and feel like to make it seem real in their young minds. Some, after weeks of therapy, would actually say they had been molested because play and fantasy the mental health workers talked to them about for six to eight weeks became real to some of them. PBS's "*Frontline*" covered this and is where to go for the graphic detail of what the young children were subjected to. Experts have suggested the best answer is to video all the exposure between the children and mental health workers not just at the end so both defense and prosecutors can question and review the whole process.

Disturbing events occurred for years starting in the late 1980s and continuing into the 1990s. One floor below the Dade County State Attorney's Office was the medical part of the jail, and an inmate with credit card numbers in his head would order merchandise for the jailers and they in turn would give him cash that he kept under his bed. They would order roses for their girlfriends or stereos and other merchandise for themselves and others. They made sure he got access to the phone, and attorneys from Janet Reno's office would go into this area of the jail as part of their duties to talk to inmates. They had to see the cash under the bed and sticking out on all sides. Cash as well as about anything else is prohibited in the jail. This was the medical part of the jail that the psychiatrist used to interview the inmates. It is difficult to believe this could go on every day for years without any of them finding out. The Miami Herald and "60 Minutes" covered this illegal activity that took place with the cooperation of the jail, Janet Reno's attorneys and the psychiatrist all participating or at least turning a blind eye for years.

In January 1990 I got into an argument with my father and was arrested and taken to Dade County Jail. It was my first arrest and the judge released me on my own recognizance in 24 hours. But as I was standing by the exit deciding where to go and how, a lady wearing a white lab coat approached me. She said they wanted to take me upstairs to talk. I knew the Dade County Attorney's Office was up there and I had been in a case several months earlier where they represented a psychiatrist that I took to court. My claim was that she did not let me visit her in person as I offered to but instead Baker-Acted me and had me picked up and brought to the same mental hospital. Janet Reno's attorneys represented her and I had sent them about fifty pages of my experience with the County Hospital (Jackson) just across the street. The doctor would never show up for the hearings and by the last time we appeared in court it was the assistant Dade County Attorney representing the hospital and the doctor all over my claim of only around one thousand dollars. My attorney dropped the claim because it was not worth pursuing any further and we had made our point. So because of this I was reluctant to go with the woman who asked me upstairs again just to talk. I gave in and rode up the elevator with the woman but she stopped at the floor below. It was the medical part of the jail. I had been tricked again. This is how I became a witness to the credit card fraud. Why they put me in there when they knew I had been writing about them was my question at first. I was held for weeks and the psychiatrists that I had taken to court showed up to interview me. The judge had a different doctor originally to interview me but his name got crossed out and Dr. Sanford Jacobson was listed. The first thing he said is that he got the letter I had written to him about my complaint against the doctor under him that I took to court. Now they had me. I had just completed a computer program a few weeks early for the surgeons at Jackson. They were going to build a trauma center, one of seven around the country. I even introduced the head surgeon I was working with to Gloria Estefan, who later did fund raising for the Trauma Center at Jackson. The surgeon who found me brought up that he dealt with psychiatrists in the hospitals and had problems with them. I only talked a few minutes with the psychiatrist and then another later. They found me incompetent to stand trial and I was sent to a long-term mental health facility where I spent nine months waiting for them to find me competent to stand trial. My father had dropped the charges before but the Dade County Attorney's Office picked them up. I was told I was being kept there because of my writing and I would not be processed out until I agreed to do a favor for the CIA. I was told to write them and I had to think up what I would do for them. After several different ideas one was accepted and the case was null prosecuted so I could do my counterintelligence work. They are just one trick after another. I had completed the work and had decided to send to the FBI and Miami Herald a copy of the court record that showed I was released on my own recognizance and a police report where the officer found me to be okay when Baker-Acting me under doctor's order. Within two weeks I was picked up again and taken to Jackson in 1992 where I met Anna Couceiro. The police report and court documents were removed from my condo and no longer exist in the court records on the case. When I went to get a copy of the police report, I was told I did not even have a file. Must be one of Janet Reno's friends in CIA investigations.

Blocking Campaign Fund Raising

Charlie Trie, a long-time friend of the Clintons with ties to the Chinese government, was under investigation by the FBI and they were about to execute a search warrant in 1997 when Janet Reno's lead attorney Laura Ingersoll, sent to Little Rock to oversee the investigation, stopped it and Trie had time to destroy and dispose of documents. In testimony to the Senate Governmental Affairs Committee, Daniel Wehr, one of the FBI agents, said the DOJ's Ms. Ingersoll told them they should not pursue any matter related to solicitation of funds for access to the President.

146

The FBI agents also complained that Ms. Ingersoll unreasonably oversaw every aspect of their investigation. She defended her actions saying the search warrant was incomplete and there was not proof. Chairman Fred Thompson did not accept her reasons and said you do not need a smoking gun to justify a search warrant. FBI agent Smith wrote Director Freeh in August 1997 complaining about the DOJ prosecutors. His comments claim their actions were not conducive to an investigation that would lead to a prosecution.

We can assume the White House does not want the Clinton's friend Charlie Trie found guilty of funneling illegal overseas money into the Clinton/Gore reelection. But did Janet Reno order this interference to block the FBI investigation and was that at the request of the President? Some would argue there is plausible cause here to investigate obstruction of justice by Janet Reno's DOJ.

Hsi Lai Temple and Al Gore

Al Gore denied even knowing the event was a fundraiser. But it has been established that he must have known. Steve Mansfield was the DOJ attorney investigating the case under Janet Reno and Radek. He was making progress and about to ask for a grand jury to convene when he was pulled off by Radek and his evidence turned over. Radek told him they were going to appoint an independent counsel and they needed him to stop so his investigation would not interfere. In testimony before Congress, Radek explained that once they pulled Steve Mansfield off they looked further and decided it was not necessary to appoint an independent counsel. Maria Hsia has been convicted on five counts for the illegal contributions at the Buddhist Temple. She is a long-time friend of Al Gore raising money for his campaigns. But Al Gore was not even questioned by Janet Reno's campaign task force until April of 2000.

By the end of June 2000 Janet Reno was called before Arlen Specter's subcommittee to answer why it had taken so long to even question Al Gore. She gave her usual answer, that it would be inappropriate to comment on a pending investigation. But she said that it was continuing and a decision to appoint an independent in light that now the new chief Robert Conard has recommended a special counsel to investigate Al Gore's fund raising during the 1996 campaign. The Republicans concluded it is now too late for an investigation to conclude before the November elections. Janet Reno's delays and blocking have worked, but are there more grounds for an investigation into her possible obstruction of justice?

LaBella and Freeh Memo Held Back

Janet Reno kept the contents of the Charles LaBella and Freeh memo a secret from Congress and the American people for two and a half years. Finally, after numerous requests and the threat of being found in contempt of Congress, she turned them over. It was known that they asked for an independent counsel. They also called for a top-to-bottom investigation of the foreign money coming into the Clinton/Gore reelection and DNC. Janet Reno's DOJ has been pursuing only the donors and not working it back to the White House. She is protecting them from being investigated and charged with taking foreign campaign contributions. Does this constitute more obstruction of justice on her part? We know there were a massive amount of different money laundering schemes to bring in the illegal contributions some have described as being analogous to how organized crime handles money. Mrs. Clinton's involvement with Johnny Chung and Charley Trie is mentioned. The possible connection between some of the donations and technology transfer to China is addressed in the memo.

Back in December 1997 Sen. Orrin Hatch wrote Louis Freeh asking him to investigate the President and Vice President for fund raising independent of Janet Reno's DOJ task force. The chairman of the Senate Judiciary Committee cited the U.S. statute which gives the authority to the attorney general and the FBI to investigate any government officer or employee for violations of the criminal code. He told Freeh that even though the attorney general is the chief law enforcement officer he had an independent obligation to ensure that the nation's laws are upheld. In May 2000 Freeh turned over memos that showed he also thought Janet Reno needed to appoint an independent counsel to ensure a proper investigation. Freeh, in a December 1996 memo, questions if the DOJ Public Integrity Section could handle the investigation and Janet Reno and Radek should step aside. FBI Deputy Director William Esposito had heard in a meeting with Radek that Janet Reno's job was on the line and passed them on to Freeh. Neil Gallagher, an FBI assistant director, testified he also heard Radek make the remarks. But Mr. Radek does not recall the meeting but is sure he did not make the comment. He admits to the DOJ being under lots of pressure at the time but it was to do a good job. Janet Reno commented publicly on these disclosures saying she never gave in to political pressure. "I call it like I see it, regardless of the consequences. I've got a month-to-month lease on my apartment, and I've been prepared to go home from the beginning," she said. But Dan Burton was not buying it, publicly announcing he was going to send over a criminal referral on the President, Vice President and Janet Reno when the next administration is in because nothing would be done if he sent it over now.

Espionage

The Central Intelligence Agency and Department of Energy reportedly discovered in 1995 that the People's Republic of China had compromised nuclear weapons design information, including that for the W-88 submarine warhead. The DOE determined this occurred between 1984 and 1988 and probably at the Los Alamos National Laboratory, although the information was available at other installations around the country. Wen-Ho Lee stood out because of the trips he and his wife made to counterparts in China. His wife worked at the lab and was active with the visiting Chinese scientist at the lab. Mr. Lee was also a suspect in an espionage investigation from 1982 to 1984. Lee proclaims his innocence and claims he only had academic contacts.

The FBI agent investigating the case asked the DOJ under the Foreign Intelligence Surveillance Act for a warrant on Lee to put him under electronic survivance and search his computer. It was denied. Such a request has never been denied to the FBI in the 20 years since the act was enacted. This and the vast amount of highly sensitive nuclear weapons secrets stolen make this very egregious. Even after Wen-Ho Lee failed lie detector tests, the FBI request for a FISC was denied by DOJ. They were turned down three times, which included a wiretap on his phone. It is known now that one of the seven tapes missing was copied after the FISC request so that copying of a complete design information on a nuclear weapons system could have been stopped. Janet Reno is accountable for turning down the requests. Did she again delay and hinder an investigation that would have been embarrassing to the President? If it got results, they would have been in the media.

Missing White House E-mail

Janet Reno is in the position of representing the President in the subpoenaed e-mails and her office is also one of the parties that subpoenaed them. How much pressure can we expect from her to recover the missing e-mails?

Judicial Watch presumes their Filegate civil lawsuit brought the missing White House e-mails to light. The e-mails had been subpoenaed by a federal grand jury and three congressional committees. Sheryl Hall, in charge of White House computer operations, said e-mail from August 1996 to November 1998 had not been stored by the mainframe because of a glitch where a filename or instruction was in lowercase and not recognized by the system that scans the hundreds of individual computer e-mails around the White House. Therefore, thousands of e-mails were never turned over to a federal grand jury, the Senate Judiciary Committee, the Senate Governmental Affairs Committee, the House Government Reform Committee or Kenneth Starr. Investigations affected include insight into Monica Lewinsky's relationship with Bill Clinton, improper use of F.B.I. files and questionable campaign fund raising.

It is also federal law that the White House must keep all e-mail and other correspondence as public record. In Congressional hearings five employees of Northrop Grumman who maintain the computers testified they had been threatened by the White House to keep the missing e-mails a secret even from the supervisors at Northrop. Robert Haas said he was told "There would be a jail cell with my name on it." Betty Lambuth said she was told not to talk to anyone, not even her spouse. "They did tell me if I did talk, my staff would be fired and they would go to jail." Mark Lindsay of the White House, in questioning about the threats, states, "I unequivocally deny that I threatened anyone regarding disclosure of the e-mail situation." His counterpart Laura Callahan blamed the threatened employees' recollections or their overactive imaginations. The White House says they discovered the problem in May 1998 and no attempt has been reported that an effort was made to recover the e-mail or notify the parties that had subpoenaed the e-mail. Is this more obstruction of justice? On March 23, 2000, the chief of the Justice Department's Campaign Finance Task Force, Robert Conrad Jr., reported that his task force had begun a criminal investigation into the subpoenaed White House e-mail and if people were threatened to keep their existence quiet. A request was also entered in U.S. District Court to delay the civil suit involving the e-mail sought by Judicial Watch. In February 2000, Jerry Seper of the Washington Times first reported the e-mail computer glitch. The White House has attributed its failure to report the problem to an innocent mistake. We know from Congressional hearings that revealed employees were threatened to keep it a secret and White House internal memos showed an effort was made to keep it quiet. There was also no effort to try to recover any of the subpoenaed e-mail. Beth Nolan, representing the White House, told Congress that all the e-mail would be recovered by the end of September and would cost $3 million. Work had already begun. But a month later, in May, Eric Duong of the company contracted by the White House said it will not be completed until Thanksgiving and found 4,925 White House backup tapes, about 600 from Al Gore, who has a separate system.

On May 4, 2000, Charles Ruff testified before the House Government Reform Committee that he first became aware of the problem in June 1998 but denied any effort to hide the missing e-mail that was under subpoena. In questioning by the committee he could not recall almost two dozen times. But the White House removed mention of the e-mail problem from Mark Lindsay's preparations for appropriations at the time before he was to ask for money to fix the problem. Lindsay was the person who notified Mr. Ruff. It is also known from a February 5, 1999, memo of Karl Hessner that addresses the extent of the missing e-mail before the end of the impeachment trial in the Senate and how it would be better not to have this brought to the attention of Congress. "Let sleeping dogs lie." Dan Burton, head of the committee, told them they did discuss this issue and they decided it was better not to ask Congress for funds to fix it, in order to keep it a secret.

Afterward

In conjunction with trying to have visitations with my son. I am also trying to be a father to my daughter who was kept a secret from me till she was sixteen. It was on my way home from the beach where I had just seen Anna. Chelsea and Shawn on the beach and talked to my son for the first time. I stopped at the grocery store on the way home thinking about Anna and the children. I only had a few items but the speed lane was long so I moved over one where I saw a young girl looking at me. She looked like an old girl friend. I said you are one of Cathy's daughters. She smiled. As I got closer I started seeing some of my features on her. The cashier was troubled that I was talking with such a young girl. So I said, "She's my daughter." She bagged her own groceries and said she would wait outside. I hurried and went outside to see her. She did most of the talking. Telling me how she had been checking up and following me to see if she wanted me as a father. She said she saw her (Anna) and liked having a brother related to the president. She also stated she knew what it was like to grow up without a father and they better not be keeping him from us. She told me how her and her mother had stopped by my place when I was in the hospital to see how they could help, mentioning the my condos president name. She told me she had permission to be with me at the beach and to go she would know and we could visit.

I would go as she said and a young girl would be there on roller skates. She would leave as I got off the beach and go right by me as I walk off. Often I would say something. She seemed pleased and content with that and would continue on her way. Once I followed her a way on foot and noticed someone waiting for her, I knew she was ok and doing well. I tried going to her mother's house, as she had asked, but there was never a car out front. I noticed a dog two doors down, it looked just like the small dog in one of Mariah Carey's videos. I stopped and talked to a man at the house. He said he watched her grow up and she had completed voice lessons and had worked hard. He also mentioned she was modeling herself after Liz Menely and it was a high goal but sometimes they make it.

It was a difficult situation having children from two different women. I made more of an effort at first to see my daughter and her mother because Anna had thoughts psychiatric doctors were too rough on me. But after the July and August, 1996 hospitalization. I never saw her on the beach again and the neighbors said they had moved. I had gotten a few letters though, and a phone call Christmas Eve from my daughter. I still do not know her first name. She told me the one time we talked not to move so she could find me in the future. So I have concentrated of my son and Anna.

I

Appendix A

July 28th 1995

Owners
Lock Town, Inc.
20201 N.W. 37th Ave.
Miami, Fl. 33056

Owners:

This week of July 1995, I was asked to have coffee at a local shop. It was a visit from the persistent Lock Town. At the end of a short stop. Karen asked me if I was using drugs. The other party immediately said you don't ask that in a public place. I had noticed that the people next to us heard. And I had said you're asking me about narcotics. I had cautioned her in private once about this subject. Then she immediately looked at her associate, implying that I don't have to answer to you. And stated where others could hear that she thinks I am using drugs. I repeated loudly and started to leave, that stuff is narcotics. The waitress had already started over and told us all not to come back. There was someone in, there that knew me. He has subsequently told me he heard. Including what was said when I was out side for a moment because we were on our way out. And I returned to see what was holding this up. I consider this slander and possibly libelous to my reputation in this community two blocks from my residence. I expect a written retraction of this and a previous statement that was put in writing. That I am a suspected of being a drug user.

I am currently checking since this is the second incident. If the context of these allegations in a meeting, meets the legal definition of blackmail.

I have also heard twice now at least that other employees of yours think she might not be safe in terms of sex. She has been here more times than I can count by herself without giving me any notice. And this is one of the reasons I wanted this to stop in the past. Now this should be taken as written notice not to send her or any other employee of Lock Town on these private premises.

This should be considered a written notice not to contact me by phone or in person. This is private property and any employee of Lock Town is asked to stay off.

Sincerely;

_____

Jerry Kletke

Appendix B

IN THE CIRCUIT COURT OF THE SEVENTEENTH
JUDICIAL CIRCUIT, IN AND FOR BROWARD
COUNTY, FLORIDA

JERRY KLETKE,	:	
PETITIONER	:	Case No. 96015756
	:	
AND	:	
	:	
ANNA COUCEIRO,	:	
RESPONDENT	:	

Respondent in pro-per-persona for answer to the petitioners Paternity and Visitation and State.

1. The petitioner claims that he is the father of my minor child, born in 1993, and that there is a Birth Certificate copy of which was allegedly to be attached to the complaint. Such alleged Birth Certificate was not attached.

The respondent categorically denies ever having sexual relations with the petitioner, and she does not have a three year old child. She has one daughter, age Eight, born of her marriage.

The respondent briefly met petitioner in her professional capacity as a Registered Nurse. The respondent believes that the petitioner is emotionally unbalanced, and is using the Judicial System to harass her, and embarrass her in making a completely unfounded claim of Paternity for a child that does not exist.

He has obtained a check off petition which provided him with inappropriate easy access to this court so that he could file a frivolous suit. Furthermore., the petitioner has filed an affidavit of insolvency and was able to obtain free processing and filing fees, which has enabled him to file a false and vexatious law suit with little or no expense. The petitioners affidavit of insolvency shows that he is not insolvent.

My mother has received treating and annoying telephone calls from the petitioner. I am in fear of him because of his mental problems. A portion of which is indicated by his bringing suit for visitation of a child that does not exist.

I ask the court to dismiss this law suit and to enter a restraining order which will prohibit the petitioner from visiting, calling or otherwise harassing and annoying me.

I hereby certify that I mailed a copy to the petitioner at: 1304 N.E. 191st Street, Apt. 333, Skylake, Florida, 33179.

Anna Couceiro, Respondent

Comment: This response was prepared before the court hearing. In court, it was shown that there was a relationship. Annas own words, "He is just like his son, what do I need him for." show there is a male child. Mrs. Clinton's mother own words: "All this because of your bastard son." I need proof in writing in order to prevail in this case. This document, along with false statements

V

under oath, is evidence of their lack of respect for the court and the truth. The errors like spelling were kept in for authenticity. I am sure an attorney prepared this like they said. This is the only material I have received in writing.

VII

Appendix C

July 1997

F.B.I.
16320 NW 2nd Ave
Miami, Fl. 33169

To: F.B.I.

I am writing because it has been six months since a simple visitation and child support hearing in Broward where Anna and her mother showed up. The court has refused my request to ask for a birth certificate for my son (Shawn). At this point and attorneys agree if there is or is not a birth certificate does not change the fact that their is a male child that Anna Couciero of Hollywood, Florida and a Jackson student nurse at the time. In the hearing see inclosed account of the hearing. Since the hearing I have continued to write and more people have check my claim and found that I have been telling the truth, they could not even believe Mr. Clinton had a Sister or mother I.C. living here.

Now my Dr. Sabas is telling me I will not see my son and I don't have one. The visit with her before this last she explained to me there is a coverup. I thought she was kidding, since it is all around this community and I over a year ago talked on the phone and sent letters to the Hill to Lott and to others.

So I asked about my son this last visit to Dr. Sabas (July 1, 1997). And she increased my medication. Told me to be back in three weeks. She threw the State Hospital at me and I responded I know what states are in computers.

VIII

And told her of contacts and some work I have done over the years. She said well kill you. I continued and included contacting the F.B.I. she then said I'll be killed on the operating table. In this I said what is stopping me from going to the republican party and having them find me a lawyer. (I checked and found the July 10th meeting at Airport Holiday is open.)

Because so many people now know Anna gave birth to Shawn. I now have tape recordings of people that know and have cared for him. And at Thanksgiving of 1996 said she would not mind having another and if I can come up with 100,000 dollars. She the mother would give me my son. I believe from conversations with the Clintons last year and what was said on T.V. as to them "adopting him" that Ms. Clinton would try and block such a money for child. They want to raise him in Little Rock so they have something to due. I plain in my next correspondence with the White House to suggest that both my son and his sister of eight spend time in the summers with the Clintons. And my daughters family said that they better not be holding out for money. But a mildly successful shareware program on the web. or a book that does well could well bring in that much. Obviously, the software solution is less political. But I am working on both. I remind myself that Anna handling and hiding of a child is not new to South Florida. And the State of Florida has Laws to handle these type of situations. But, if I prove in court, then Anna and her Mother would clearly be guilty of making serious false statement under oath. Although the thought sometimes of Anna spending a week or two in jail. And she could get much more. Some times appeals to me. But, I hope for change in her as she has done in the past. Just the going though nursing school late in life and she agrees with me that I would be good for her daughter too. For at least a few years until maybe my son is older. I will continue to slowly but with effort write and talk with curtain people. Like, Mr. and Mrs. Clinton by mail. I think Mrs. Clinton would like to raise my son in Arkansas without me.

The last thing I told her is I don't go to meetings. Although I use to work for private Clubs in this Town. And by the way, they both have offered me a chance to go back. I keep to myself and a lot of people in this town have trusted me for years.

I am enclosing what is on file in court as to doctors' conversations since I went out with Anna. This was not read by Judge Greene until after the ruling. He made it clear that I could refile.

Sincerely;

_____

Jerry Kletke
Programmer/writer

Appendix D
51 Questions for the President and First Lady
November 20, 1998

1. Do you and Hillary think I love my son, Shawn?

2. Does Shawn keep asking for his father?

3. Did you and Hillary still plan to "adopt" him?

4. When did you plan to tell me, his father, that he existed?

5. Have you covered up the existence of Shawn?

6. Isn't it an obstruction of justice in a civil case to have me Baker-Acted to stop or delay my seeking due process under the law?

7. Did you or Hillary help Anna prepare the written response to my claim in the January 1997 child visitation and support case?

8. Did you or Hillary instruct Anna to lie under oath in this civil case?

9. Did you know Anna was a cocaine trafficker in the 1980s in South Florida?

10. Did you know she and her boyfriend trafficked in cocaine in California as a way to have cocaine and money too?

11. Did you know she wanted me to traffic cocaine and distribute it to doctors in Miami?

12. Did you know she got upset and left when I refused?

13. Did you know I tried to stop her cocaine traffic by going to the FBI?

14. Did you tell Anna you would get me if something came of it?

15. Did you know that at the trial Anna brought up cocaine trafficking?

16. Did you and Hillary know there was a arrest of a male using her address with cocaine on him?

17. Did you know the first time I called Anna in 1996 I got a male and said I did not want Anna for romanic reasons but want to see my son?

18. Do you know the second time I talked to him, he said, "You know what I could do to him?" (my son)

19. Do you and Hillary know Anna and her sister who have picked up my son from the day care have a homosexual relationship?

20. Do you and Hillary think a gay homosexual relationship is good for my son?

21. Do you have any reason why I would not be good for Shawn my son?

22. Have you and Hillary or Anna ever used the CIA to help keep me from seeking due process under Florida State Law?

23. Have you or Hillary ever tried to stop the print or video media from running my story?

24. Did you know Madonna knew of my son when we were on Miami Beach together?

25. Did Hillary and Janet Reno ever fly into Miami to stop the press on Madonna and me?

26. Did you or Hillary ever talk to Dr. Glassman about me and Shawn?

27. Did you tell Dr. Glassman to have me stop seeing Madonna?

28. Did Hillary ever say that since I would not let you adopt my son, I would marry Anna?

29. Does or did Anna ever want to get married?

30. Do you or Hillary have any objection to my helping Anna get into a townhouse?

31. Where is my son at night?

32. Did you know Anna's next-door neighbor never sees my son but does see his sister?

33. Bill and Hillary, did you take my son Shawn to New England with you when you were there with Walter Cronkite just before your Russia visit?

34. Do you know Hillary was the instigator behind many of these illegal activities?

35. As chief law enforcement officer, are you interfering with Florida State Law in this matter?

36. As President of the United States, is Anna with the CIA like she said?

37. As President of the United States have you or though Hillary used this influence to get Lock Town or Jackson to have me committed?

38. Did you or your wife talk with Dr. Master or Carter about this matter?

39. Did you or Hillary talk with Dr. A. Cohen about me or Shawn?

40. Did you know my son said you were a big man as he motioned with his arms that you picked him up?

41. Do you or Hillary know Anna scared me away from Shawn, my son, on Miami Beach by saying "doctor, doctor?"

42. Do you know Anna has slept with most of the doctors in the psychiatric section of Jackson?

43. Did you ok or order the implants put in at Jackson Hospital were Anna worked, in both my ears?

44. Did or does Anna use this for political purposes to have me hospitalized in the past to keep me from seeing my son as Florida State Law allows?

45. Did you know Dr. Baron who works with Anna at Jackson and talked about Anna, me and Shawn in 1998?

46. Did you or Hillary take money that you knew came from Chinese business or military interests?

47. Did you consider this money in transferring technology that can be used by the Chinese military.

48. In one of your phone calls in 1996 to me did you expect to be impeached at that time because you said you did not know how long you would be here?

49. Hillary did in one of your phone calls to me in 1996 say? "You have already been told you are going to be impeached. But you were going to win. The White House is a beautiful place to get back at our enemies."

50. Hillary, do you and your family in South Florida plan to raise Shawn with out his father as you have since 1993?

51. Do you or Hillary think a second independent counsel should be set up to investigate these matters?

Appendix E

A few love poems for Hillary that I would include in letters to the Clintons.

Your Ever Lasting Love

Your Love is Ever Lasting.

It is with me where ever I go.

Your Love never leaves me.

So when are you going to tell the World we are in Love.

The Pleasure of Love

Your Love brings me endless end less pleasure.

I an lost with your Love.

May are Love last forever.

My eyes are blue my lips are red

But before I kiss you I will turn you into the Feds.

Projects:

Office Expeditor: Calendar, Mailer, Rolodex, Index Cards MS-DOS also Forms And Labels Generator an add on to Office Expeditor(R). Source code in 'C' run under Dos #.x or greater.

Inventory/Sales, Accounting/Package, Payroll Programs.

In MS-Basic 4 This I would use to customize for small business that had a need for unique functions. Like a 135 char printouts or special searches and sorts. MS DOS Basic.

A mail merge written for Apple II Apple Writer that could also handle Math Formulas. Presented this at F.I.U. auditorium before Apple Works was released. Apple Basic, Microsoft Compiler Copyrighted 1984, before Apple Works was released. Demonstrated at Apple Business Meeting at F.I.U. main campus.

Education:

University of South Florida - 1973-77 Biology Major 3.5 yrs.

The College Register Rec. in 1977 Top 2% in Nation

Undergraduate Research Dr. Web and Rex Lee (1976-77).

Several publications within a year. In 1972, an associate of Dr. Web received the Nobel Price for work on the same equipment. I did not know until I worked for part time for 9 months.

About The Author

The author is a student of Biology and Computers. Meeting friends that were interested in politics and when on to work for the government, in collage. His first book on Biology and future developments, with projections. Has held up well over time.

Writing computer programs for business and technical applications, for over ten years. Some work on programs for analysis of DNA used, in DNA finger printing. Design and wrote the code for Surgical Trauma Centers around the country. And automated Credit Bureau process.

With friends and an interest in politics. Was exposed to the inside of the process. At times working with active democrats. Now, just after being exposed to the very liberal relatives of Hillary. Is a conservative republican.

University of Miami	1978-79 Computer Sci. 15 hrs. half the curriculum for B.S.
Florida International Univ.	1986-88 Computer Science/Bio.One Course from graduation. It is best because I helped raise funds for Science Depts.

Languages:

MS-basic with while statements, 'C++' Borland Professional. Pascal, Fortran VII, very rusty Cobol, and Assembly Macros.

In Who's Who in America, Sceince and Engineering.

Have read over 50 non-science works.

www.ingramcontent.com/pod-product-compliance
Lightning Source LLC
Chambersburg PA
CBHW030441290526
45786CB00001B/395